ITIL® 4 Exam Prep

Questions, Answers & Explanations

ITIL® is a registered trademark of AXELOS Limited.
The Swirl logo™ is a trademark of AXELOS Limited.

Ready to take the real ITIL Exam from your own computer?

Looking for ITIL courses and exam prep tools?

Visit us at www.PMTraining.com

PMtraining™ Get ITIL Certified Today

Get the Course with Certification Exam Included!

Our On-Demand ITIL Foundation course bundle effectively prepares students for all topic areas of the certification exam.

*Now offering **the real ITIL certification exam online!***

An ITIL Curriculum Focused on Exam Success

Built around accelerated learning techniques and carefully designed learning materials, this intense, focused ITIL training delivers a passing ITIL® Exam score on your very first try.

Course Developed by Accredited Training Organization

All ITIL courses offered by PMTraining are accredited by Axelos as licensed ITIL training organization

Live Instructors to Answer Questions

Students receive access to instructors who will answer course and ITIL questions.

Studio-Quality ITIL Lessons Available On-Demand

Each course milestone contains multiple instructor sessions designed for On-Demand learning.

Credits and PDUs Earned

This course is an officially licensed ITIL product, and is accredited by ITIL Exam Institute, PEOPLECERT.

ITIL 4 Certification Exam Included, Schedule Online

Upon course completion, schedule your ITIL 4 Foundation exam online. The cost of the the exam is included in this course!

Printable ITIL Study Guide and Workbook

A detailed, printable ITIL Study Guide and course workbook is included as a supplement to the course. The ITIL Study Guide summarizes each course

TRAINING ORGANIZATION ACCREDITED BY

PEOPLECERT ON BEHALF OF AXELOS

Start Today or Learn More

info@pmtraining.com

1-800-581-9819

www.PMTraining.com

I passed today. You have another ITIL success to add to your alumni list.

Professional. Measurable. Realistic.

ITIL® Exam Prep

Questions, Answers & Explanations

Christopher Scordo, PMP, ITIL

Power Your Career

www.PMTraining.com

Copyrighted Material

© Copyright 2020 by SSI Logic. Printed and bound in the United States of America. All rights reserved. No part of this book may be reproduced or transmitted in any form or by any means, electronic or mechanical, or incorporated into any information retrieval system, electronic or mechanical, without the written permission of the copyright owner.
2020 Edition.

Although the author and publisher of this work have made every effort to ensure accuracy and completeness of content entered in this book, we assume no responsibility for errors, inaccuracies, omissions, or inconsistencies included herein. Any similarities of people, places, or organizations are completely unintentional.

Published by SSI Logic

ISBN-13: 9781676909736

All inquiries should be addressed via email to:
support@ssilogic.com

or by mail post to:
SSI Solutions, INC
340 S Lemon Ave #9038
Walnut, CA 91789

ITIL® is a registered trademark of AXELOS Limited.

Copyright © AXELOS Limited 2018 All rights reserved.
Material is reproduced under license from AXELOS

Table of Contents

Introduction

    Welcome 2

    ITIL Foundation Exam Overview 4

Practice Exams and Quizzes

    ITIL Foundation Mock Exam (LITE) - 1 . *WEEK 5* . . 6

    Knowledge Area Quiz: General Management Practices *WEEK 5* . 20

    ITIL Foundation Mock Exam (LITE) - 2 . *WEEK 5* . 25

    ✓ Knowledge Area Quiz: Generic Concepts and Definitions. *WEEK 5* . 40 *8/10*

    ITIL Foundation Mock Exam (LITE) - 3. *WEEK 6* . . 45

    Knowledge Area Quiz: ITIL Concepts . *WEEK 5* . . 59

    ITIL Foundation Mock Exam (LITE) - 4. *WEEK 7* . . 63

    Knowledge Area Quiz: Service Management Practices *WEEK 6* . 77

    ITIL Foundation Mock Exam (LITE) - 5 . *WEEK 7* . . 82

    Knowledge Area Quiz: Service Value Chain (SVC) *WEEK 3* . 97

    ITIL Foundation Mock Exam (LITE) - 6 . *WEEK 7* . . 101

    ITIL Foundation Mock Exam (LITE) - 7 . *WEEK 8* . . 116

    ITIL Foundation Mock Exam (LITE) - 8. *WEEK 8* . . 130

    Knowledge Area Quiz: Service Value System (SVS). *WEEK 2* . 144

    ITIL Foundation Mock Exam (LITE) - 9 . *WEEK 8* . . 148

    Knowledge Area Quiz: Technical Management Practices . *WEEK 6* . 163

    ITIL Foundation Mock Exam (LITE) - 10. *WEEK 8* . . 168

Quick ITIL 4 Exam Quiz (I)	181
ITIL Foundation Mock Exam (LITE) - 11.	186
Quick ITIL 4 Exam Quiz (II)	200
ITIL Foundation Mock Exam (LITE) - 12.	205
ITIL Foundation Mock Exam (LITE) -13.	219
ITIL Foundation Mock Exam (LITE) -14.	233
ITIL Foundation Mock Exam (LITE) -15.	245
ITIL Foundation Mock Exam (LITE) - 16.	258

Glossary

ITIL 4 Glossary and Key Terms.	270

Additional Resources

Exam Taking Tips.	292

INTRODUCTION

Welcome

Thank you for selecting PMTraining's *ITIL® Exam Prep – Questions, Answers, and Explanations* for your ITIL Foundation study needs. The goal of this book is to provide full mock exams and practice tests which allow you to become comfortable with the pace, subject matter, and difficulty of the ITIL 4 Foundation exam.

In this edition of the text, question explanations have been updated to reinforce ITIL concepts; content improvements have been further applied to reflect the ITIL 4 Foundation exam as of January 2020.

The content in this book is designed to optimize the time you spend studying in multiple ways.

1. Practice exams in this book reflect the actual length and subject matter of the ITIL Foundation exam and are designed to be completed in one hour; allowing you to balance your time between practice tests and offline study.

2. Passing score requirements in this book are slightly higher than the real exam; allowing you to naturally adjust to a higher test score requirement.

3. Practice exams included in this book cover the entire scope of the ITIL 4 Foundation syllabus and ITIL Service Value System (SVS), while shorter quizzes focus only on specific knowledge areas.

The practice exam content in this book is structured into two general types of exam preparation:

- Mock exams which allow you to test your knowledge across multiple iterations of the ITIL Foundation exam; designed to be completed within one hour.

- Knowledge Area Quizzes, which reflect brief practice tests focused on specific ITIL Foundation syllabus areas; designed to be completed in 10 to 20 minutes.

We wish you the best of luck in your pursuit of the ITIL Foundation certificate.

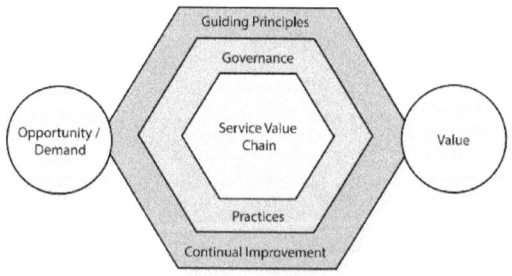

Diagram: ITIL Service Value System – Reproduced under license from AXELOS

ITIL® Foundation Exam Overview

The ITIL practice questions in this book reflect the ITIL 4 Foundation exam curriculum centered around the overall Service Value System (SVS).

About the IT Infrastructure Library (ITIL) Foundation Certification

As of 2018, the ITIL certification has been owned and managed by the accrediting body known as AXELOS through a joint venture with the UK Cabinet Office. AXELOS provides licensing of ITIL intellectual property to various organizations, licenses and accredits Examination Institute (EIs), and provides overall management and updates to the ITIL framework.

The overall ITIL certification scheme relies on the ITIL Foundation certificate as the first core requirement prior to attaining advanced ITIL certifications. Further, ITIL offers two separate certification "streams" once the Foundation is attained, they are: the *ITIL 4 Managing Professional (ITIL MP)* stream and the *ITIL 4 Strategic Leader (ITIL SL)* stream. The *ITIL Master* designation is the highest level of ITIL designation available to attain.

ITIL Foundation Exam Details

The ITIL Foundation exam is designed to objectively assess and measure knowledge reflecting ITIL holistic approach to service management. This holistic approach, known as the "Service Value System" (SVS) represents the integration of all components and activities of an organization working together, in order to facilitate the creation of value.

The actual ITIL exam itself is offered in a computer based testing (CBT) environment through a single Examination Institute (EI) known as PeopleCert. PeopleCert offers ITIL Foundation exams which reflect the predefined Foundation syllabus; with little or no variation between the exams they administer. Exams are primarily taken via an Online Proctor (OLP) format due to student convenience, but may also be taken in-person at a proctored testing center.

A summary of the exam structure and passing requirements are as follows:

- There are 40 total multiple choice questions which make up the ITIL Foundation exam
- Individuals have 60 minutes to complete the exam
- Individuals must score 65% or higher to pass the exam (26 of 40 questions)

The ITIL Foundation Syllabus

The ITIL Foundation syllabus reflects the subject matter areas covered in the exam, and is comprised broadly of the components which holistically apply to the Service Value System (SVS).

To simplify matters, ITIL defines 34 management practices which are categorized in to three general categories. These categories, covered at a summary level on the exam, are:

- General Management Practices
- Service Management Practices
- Technical Management Practices

The ITIL practice exam content in this book include practice quizzes targeted at each of the general ITIL Management Practices, in addition to the Service Value System (SCS); the Service Value Chain (SVC); and Generic Concepts and Definitions.

The ITIL Certification Scheme

The hierarchy of available ITIL certifications is known as the *ITIL certification scheme*. As mentioned earlier, the entry level for the scheme is the ITIL Foundation certification. Once the ITIL Foundation Level is successfully completed, the candidate becomes eligible to take further ITIL certifications within the scheme.

As noted earlier, two separate ITIL certification "streams" are available to professionals who have attained the ITIL Foundation level.

These two streams allow individuals to focus on areas of their profession in a more specialized manner, and are known as:

- *ITIL 4 Managing Professional (ITIL MP)* stream
- *ITIL 4 Strategic Leader (ITIL SL)* stream

The ITIL MP stream targets those professionals who work within "technology and digital teams across businesses"; while the ITIL SL stream focuses on the development of business strategy with regard to digitally enabled services. Both streams include multiple "modules" that ensure specialization and complete understanding.

The highest level of the ITIL qualification scheme is the *ITIL Master Level*. This is the final qualification available within the ITIL certification scheme and is reserved for those professionals who have demonstrated evidence of their ability to successfully implement ITIL framework concepts and best practices in their profession.

Practice Exams and Quizzes

ITIL Foundation Mock Exam (LITE) - 1

Test Name: ITIL Foundation Mock Exam (LITE) - 1
Total Questions: 40
Correct Answers Needed to Pass: 30 (75.00%)
Time Allowed: 60 Minutes

Test Description

This is a cumulative ITIL Foundation test which can be used as a baseline for initial performance. This practice test includes questions from all ITIL question categories.

Test Questions

1. A customer calls in to the Delta Solutions Service Desk to have his Intranet password reset. Since he had three failed login attempts, the Intranet system locked him out. What term best reflects this type of customer request?

    A. Service Request

    B. Request for Change (RFC)

    C. Minor Incident

    D. Error Call

2. What term best reflects a Service Management product's ability to be substantially enlarged, either via the amount of data it stores, or via the number of users it supports?

    A. Security

    B. Capacity

    C. Scalability

    D. Continuity

3. What concept below reflects "fitness for purpose" and represents the characteristics of a service which enables a customer to achieve their desired outcomes?

    A. Warranty

    B. Service Management

    C. Resources

    D. Utility

4. Shock, avoidance, blame, self-blame, and acceptance are phases of what event?

A. Service Failure

B. Emotional Change Cycle *(circled)*

C. Damage Control

D. Emergency Rollback

5. Which Guiding Principle recommends organizing tasks into iterations.

   A. Keep it Simple

   B. Collaborate and promote visibility

   C. Start where you are

   D. Progress iteratively with feedback *(circled)*

6. In the RACI model, what role represents the people who are kept updated on the progress of activities?

   A. Informed *(circled)*

   B. Responsible

   C. Accountable

   D. Consulted

7. What Service Management Practice quantifies the financial value of IT service assets which underlie the provisioning of services, and the qualifications of operational forecasting?

   A. Portfolio Management *(circled)*

   B. Demand Management

   C. Strategy Management

   D. Service Financial Management

8. Which of the items below holds together any and all information on relevant CIs, along with their related attributes, in a centralized location; and can link to Incident, Problem, and Change records?

   A. Definitive Media Store

   B. Service Configuration Management System

   C. Asset Management System

   D. Discovery, Deployment, and Licensing Technologies *(circled)*

9. Select the best terms to fill in the blanks: The _____ is a subset of the _____ and only includes services which are approved and active in Service Operation.

ITIL Foundation Mock Exam (LITE) 1 - Practice Questions

A. Product/Service Portfolio, Business Catalogue

B. Configuration Management System, Service Portfolio

C. Service Catalogue, Product/Service Portfolio

D. Product/Service Portfolio, Service Catalogue

10. Business Impact Analysis involves identifying the critical business functions within the organization and determining the impact of failure to perform the business function beyond the maximum acceptable outage. What types of criteria can be used to evaluate this impact?

A. Policy and process

B. Internal and external risks

C. Exposure and liability

D. Customer service and finance

11. Which of the following statements are TRUE with respect to the Service Catalog? I) The Service Catalog documents the actual and present capabilities of the service provider. II) The Service Catalog enables the service provider to customize service solutions for any customer.

A. I only

B. None of these statements are true

C. I and II

D. II only

12. What are the two main characteristics of service assets?

A. Internal and External

B. Utility (Fit for Purpose) and Warranty (Fit for Use)

C. Shared and Exclusive

D. Outsourced and rented

13. Normally, Risk is perceived as a negative state, but some risks can be a/an _____ .

A. Positive

B. Advantage

C. Improvement

D. Opportunity

14. Charging customers a specific dollar amount for services received is standard operating procedure with commercial service providers. In shared service arrangements, where the provider and the customer may be part of the same company, organization, or division, direct payment of costs by customer to service provider is not as common. What is one way of handling this type of arrangement?

A. Accrual accounting

B. Notional charging

C. Indirect costs

D. RFC management

15. An effective approach to an undertaking which has already proven to be successful, but has not yet become common industry practice, is known as what?

A. Best Practice

B. Generally Accepted Principles

C. Perceived Wisdom

D. Good Practice

16. Deming's PDCA tool is used to manage which ITIL Practice?

A. Continual Improvement

B. Service Continuity Management

C. Service Configuration Management

D. Availability Management

17. What role is responsible for managing the work of 1st line support staff, and managing Major Incidents as they occur?

A. Incident Manager

B. Alert Manager

C. Problem Manager

D. Event Manager

18. An item such as a service component or an asset of the organization which is under the control of Configuration Management is known as what?

A. Resource

B. Variant

ITIL Foundation Mock Exam (LITE) 1 - Practice Questions

C. Configuration Management System (CMS)

D. Service Configuration Item

19. Which item below best reflects a group, team, or person that performs tasks relevant to a specific activity?

    A. Best Practice

    B. Role

    C. Function

    D. Service

20. TechCo, an IT service provider, strives to focus heavily on where and how to compete in the market; distinguish its capabilities from its competitors; and view the services it provides as a strategic asset which must be constantly improved. What Practice analyzes these goals?

    A. Continual Improvement

    B. Service Transition

    C. Service Design

    D. Strategy Management

21. In which ITIL Practice Category is Supplier Management executed?

    A. General Management practices

    B. Continual Improvement Practice

    C. Service Management practice

    D. Service Design Practice

22. Which of the following are the CORRECT choices for the stages in Deming Quality Cycle?

    A. Plan-Do-Check-Act

    B. Process-Do-Check-Audit

    C. Plan-Data-Check-Act

    D. Produce-Data-Correct-Audit

23. Which of the following statements are TRUE with respect to an Event in the Event Management Practices? I) The occurrence of an Event can have considerable significance on the infrastructure and IT service delivery. II) Events are notifications created by a CI (Configuration Item) or IT service or a software tool. III) Events can be monitored using active and passive monitoring tools.

A. II only

B. I, II

C. I

D. II, III *(circled)*

24. The SMART model is used to elaborate:

    A. Requirements

    B. SLAs

    C. Organizational goals *(circled)*

    D. Processes

25. Which of the following statements is false regarding Service Configuration Management?

    A. A Configuration Structure represents the relationships between all Configuration Items (CIs) within a given configuration. *(circled)*

    B. A Configuration Management Database (CMDB) may contain one or many Configuration Management Systems (CMSs)

    C. Ensuring the proper management of Configuration Items (CIs) is the responsibility of the Configuration Control activity under Service Transition.

    D. A Configuration Management Database (CMDB) stores the attributes and relationships of Configuration Items (CIs) within the organization.

26. Which of the following are valid objectives of the ITIL Service Desk Practice?   a. To quickly restore normal service to users after an interruption   b. To provide first-line support to users   c. To manage the resolution of incidents   d. To escalate requests which cannot be resolved by first-line support

    A. B, C, D

    B. A, B

    C. A, B, D *(circled)*

    D. All these responses / All of the above

27. DataCorp provides webhosting services to all its subsidiaries through its internal IT division. This is an

ITIL Foundation Mock Exam (LITE) 1 - Practice Questions

example of what type of Service Provider?

A. Type II

B. Outsourcing

C. Managed Hosting

D. Expansion-based

28. From the customer's perspective, what are the two most important components which make up the value of a service?

A. Utility and Warranty

B. Resources and Capabilities

C. Design and Capacity

D. Utility and Resources

29. Which ITIL Practice attempts to find the balance between resources, capabilities, and demand?

A. Supplier Management

B. Financial Management for IT Services

C. Service Level Management

D. Capacity & Performance Management

30. Aristotle Publishing has decided to implement a shared services model for their IT infrastructure. In which ITI Practice will the shared services design team ask the question "Why do we need this Service?"

A. Service Design

B. Strategy Management

C. Service Level Management

D. Continual Improvement

31. What model, utilized under Continual Improvement, consists of six steps which include embracing the vision, assessing the current situation, agreeing on priorities, planning to achieve quality, taking action, verifying metrics, and ensuring momentum for improvement is maintained?

A. ITIL Continual Improvement Model

B. Deming Cycle

C. PDCA Model

D. Service Lifecycle

32. A large storage array has been installed to support a new digital locker service offered by coblus.com. Which of the following terms best describes this array?

   A. Resource

   B. SAN

   C. NAS *(circled)*

   D. Hardware

33. A technique used in managing Incidents is called _____. It involves gathering stakeholders from different areas of support sharing ideas, each leaving the group when it becomes apparent that their skills will not help resolve the Incident.

   A. Service Continuity Planning

   B. Known Error Management

   C. Problem Solving

   D. Swarming *(circled)*

34. Gary is responsible for managing the media for his organization's data backup system. The activities that he performs include changing media in the robotic tape library, ordering new media as required, and ensuring that backup media is archived according to the organization's policies. What is Gary's role?

   A. Process owner

   B. Operational owner

   C. Operational practitioner *(circled)*

   D. Practitioner

35. Hill and Meyer, LLC have purchased a 3rd party maintenance contract for 8x5x4 onsite support for specific network components to limit potential downtime in the event of an outage. What is this type of contract called?

   A. Operational Level Agreement *(circled)*

   B. Internal Service Agreement

   C. Service Level Agreement

   D. Service Agreement

36. Regarding the Service Desk, a measurement of "What percentage of calls were answered within 45 seconds?" is an example of a:

ITIL Foundation Mock Exam (LITE) 1 - Practice Questions

A. Critical Success Factor

B. Key Performance Indicator

C. High Priority

D. Best Practice

37. ITIL management practices are divided into _____ Categories.

    A. Three

    B. Four

    C. Five

    D. Two

38. When must Service Level Requirements be defined?

    A. Before the service is delivered.

    B. As part of the contract negotiation process.

    C. Every time the service is performed.

    D. After the service is delivered.

39. Charles is the new IT Manager at Global Services and one of the first projects he undertakes is the complexity of all the different elements of the organization's environment and eco systems. He realizes that he needs to establish a _____ Management Practice.

    A. Architecture Management Practice

    B. Portfolio Management Practice

    C. Infrastructure and Platform Management Practice

    D. Strategy Management Practice

40. Who issues the final decision with respect to the proposed changes to the IT infrastructure?

    A. The appropriate Change Authority

    B. The Manager who raised the change issues the final decision with respect to the Change.

    C. The Release Manager issues the final decision with respect to the Change.

    D. The Test Manager issues the final decision with respect to the Change.

ITIL Foundation Mock Exam (LITE) - 1 Answer Key and Explanations

1. A - A Service Request best reflects this customer request, as it was not caused by an underlying fault in the IT infrastructure. (ITIL Concepts) [ITIL Concepts]

2. C - This concept is best represented by the term: Scalability. (General Concepts and Definitions) [Generic Concepts and Definitions]

3. D - Utility reflects "fitness for purpose" and is what enables the customer to achieve their desired outcome. (ITIL Concepts) [ITIL Concepts]

4. B - One of the biggest causes of failure of Changes is not sufficiently considering the way in which the Changes affect people. The emotional phases that may occur before change acceptance are shock, avoidance, external blame, self-blame, and acceptance. (Service Management Practices) [Service Management Practices]

5. D - Breaking down work into small iterations can avoid re-work when the project shifts directions. (ITIL Concepts) [ITIL Concepts]

6. A - The "Informed" role of the RACI model are those people who are kept updated on the progress of activities and the project. (Generic Concepts and Definitions) [Generic Concepts and Definitions]

7. D - Financial Management is the Service Management Practice responsible for quantifying the financial value of IT services, assets, and qualifications of operational forecasting. (General Management Practices) [General Management Practices]

8. B - A Service Configuration Management Practice documents information on any and all relevant CIs, along with their related attributes, in a centralized location; and can link to Incident, Problem, and Change records. (Service Management Practices) [Service Management Practices]

9. C - The Service Catalogue is a subset of the Product/Service Portfolio and only includes services which are approved and active/live. (Service Management Practices) [Service Management Practices]

10. D - The Business Impact analysis is an essential element in the business continuity process and dictates the

strategy to be followed for risk reduction and recovery after a catastrophe. The BIA consists of two parts: investigation of the loss of a practice, and eliminating the effect of that loss. (ITIL Concepts) [ITIL Concepts]

11. C - Both statements are TRUE regarding the Service Catalog; as it reflects the actual and present capabilities of the service provider, and enables the service provider to customize service solutions for any customer. (Service Management Practices) [Scrvice Management Practices]

12. B - The two main characteristics of Service Assets are Utility (Fit for Purpose) and Warranty (Fit for Use). (Generic Concepts and Definitions) [Generic Concepts and Definitions]

13. D - There are negative risks; i.e., threats to an organization's stability. Positive risks lie with missed opportunities. (Generic Concepts and Definitions) [Generic Concepts and Definitions]

14. B - In Notional Charging, the costs incurred in the provision of a specific service are communicated to the recipient, but no payment is required. This method is useful for encouraging more efficient use of IT resources. (ITIL Concepts) [ITIL Concepts]

15. A - A proven, effective approach which is not yet industry practice is known as a Best Practice. Once it is commonly adopted industry-wide, it becomes a state of Good Practice which is continuously improved. (Generic Concept and Definitions) [Generic Concepts and Definitions]

16. A - The Plan- Do-Check-Act tool prescribes a repeating pattern of improvement efforts. (Generic Concepts and Definitions) [Generic Concepts and Definitions]

17. A - The Incident Manager is responsible for the activities above, and also maintains all relevant Incident Management systems. (Service Management Practices) [Service Management Practices]

18. D - A Configuration Item (CI) includes any item which is, or will be, under the control of Service Configuration Management. (ITIL Concepts) [ITIL Concepts]

19. B - Under ITIL, this statement best describes a Role. (ITIL Concepts) [ITIL Concepts]

20. D - Marketing focus, distinguishing one's capabilities, and performance

anatomy are all goals of Strategy Management. (Service Management Practices) [Service Management Practices]

21. A - Supplier Management is one of the General Management Practices. (General Management Practices) [General Management Practices]

22. A - The Correct activities of the Deming Cycle are: Plan-Do-Check-Act. (Generic Concepts and Definitions) [Generic Concepts and Definitions]

23. C - The following statements are true with respect to an event in the Event Management Process. I). The occurrence of an event can have considerable significance on the infrastructure and IT service delivery. (Service Management Practices) [Service Management Practices]

24. A - Every requirement must be SMART (Specific, Measurable, Achievable/ Appropriate, Realistic/ Relevant, and Timely/ time-bound) formulated. (Generic Concepts and Definitions) [Generic Concepts and Definitions]

25. B - A Service Configuration Management System may contain one or more Configuration Management Databases (CMDB), but a CMDB may not contain a CMS. All of the other statements are true. (Service Management Practices) [Service Management Practices]

26. D - All of the items listed are valid objectives of the Service Desk Practice. (Service Management Practices) [Service Management Practices]

27. A - The market of Type II Service Providers is internal to the enterprise, but it is distributed through the business units. (Service Management Practices) [Service Management Practices]

28. A - From the customer's perspective, the value of a service is represented by fitness for purpose (Utility) and fitness for use (Warranty). (ITIL Concepts) [ITIL Concepts]

29. D - The goal of Capacity and Performance Management is to ensure the current and future capacity and performance demands of the customer regarding IT service provision are delivered against justifiable costs. (Service Management Practices) [Service Management Practices]

30. B - One of the major concepts developed is determining how to create service value. This ensures that,

before rushing out to determine how to design a service, the organization stops to ask why the service is needed. (General Management Practices) [General Management Practices]

31. A - The six steps describe the components of the Continual Improvement Model, which is an iterative improvement process under Continual Improvement. (ITIL Concepts) [ITIL Concepts]

32. A - Resources are tangible or consumable assets such as IT infrastructure used to provide a service. In this scenario, the storage array is a resource providing disc space to coblus.com customers. (ITIL Concepts) [ITIL Concepts]

33. D - Swarming is a method of troubleshooting Incidents and involves gathering stakeholders from different areas of support sharing ideas, each leaving the group when it becomes apparent that their skills will not help resolve the Incident. (Generic Concepts and Definitions) [Generic Concepts and Definitions]

34. D - The practitioner is responsible for performing one or more activities. This role is also responsible for ensuring inputs and outputs for the practices are correct, and creating/ managing activity records. (ITIL Concepts) [ITIL Concepts]

35. C - A contract is between an organization and an external supplier that supports the IT organization delivery services is a type of Service Level Agreement. (Service Management Practices) [Service Management Practices]

36. B - This measurement is an example of a Key Performance Indicator which would apply to the Service Desk. (Service Management Practices) [Service Management Practices]

37. A - ITIL Management Practices are divided into three categories. (ITIL Concepts) [ITIL Concepts]

38. A - In order to ensure services meet customer expectations, Service Level Requirements must be clear before the service is delivered. (ITIL Concepts) [ITIL Concepts]

39. A - Charles identified the need to establish an Architecture Management Practice to control the existing environment and to enable planning for future architecture requirements. (General Management Practices) [General Management Practices]

40. A - The appropriate Change Authority issues the final decision with respect to the Change. (Service Management Practices) [Service Management Practices]

Knowledge Area Quiz: General Management Practices

Test Name: Knowledge Area Quiz: General Management Practices
Total Questions: 10
Correct Answers Needed to Pass: 7 (70.00%)
Time Allowed: 10 Minutes

Test Description

This practice test specifically targets the subject area of Service Management as a Practice.

Test Questions

1. What are the fundamental activities for Service Financial Management?

   A. Budgeting, Fiscal Responsibility, Funding

   B. Direct Costs, Cost Elements, and Cost Types

   C. Budgeting, IT Accounting, Charging

   D. Charging, Budgeting, Direct Costs

2. Which of the following are true: I) An Identity and Access Management Process is contained in the Information Security Management Practice. II) Information Security Management is a Process within the Identity and Access Management Process.

   A. Neither

   B. I and II

   C. II only

   D. I only

3. The goals of which ITIL Practice are to manage investments in service management across the enterprise and maximize their value?

   A. Capacity and performance Management

   B. Service Catalog Management

   C. Service Value Management

   D. Portfolio Management

4. Which of the following items cannot be captured in a database?

   A. Data

B. Wisdom

C. Information

D. Knowledge

5. The Knowledge Management Practice is in which ITIL Category?

   A. General Management Practices

   B. Technical Management Practices

   C. Service Management Practices

   D. Service Design

6. The main challenge in implementing Information Security Management is:

   A. Establishing clear policies

   B. Strict Change Control and Configuration Management.

   C. Ensuring adequate support for the company, business security, and senior management.

   D. Justifying the need for Information Security Management

7. What Service Management Practice focuses on the type and extent of data accessible to a user, identify of a user, and the rights of a user?

   A. Availability Management

   B. Monitoring and Event Management

   C. Incident Management

   D. Information Security Management

8. Service investments fall into which three categories?

   A. Start the business, run the business, enhance the business

   B. Transform the business, define the business, and run the business

   C. Transform the business, grow the business, and run the business

   D. Control the business, run the business, grow the business

9. Information Security Management maintains which of the following key information properties?

   A. Confidentiality, integrity, uptime

Knowledge Area Quiz: General Management Practices - Practice Questions

B. Configuration, integrity, accuracy

C. Confidentiality, integrity, availability

D. Confidentiality, intelligence, availability

10. ACME, Inc. is considering upgrading the servers that run its corporate email system and the human resources database. Due to budgetary constraints, however, only one system can be upgraded at this time. It is determined that the corporate email system will be upgraded now, and the human resources database will be upgraded at a later time. During which ITIL Practice is this decision made?

   A. Service Desk

   B. Business Analysis

   C. Deployment Management

   D. Portfolio Management

Knowledge Area Quiz: General Management Practices Answer Key and Explanations

1. C - There are three fundamental activities for Service Financial Management: budgeting, IT accounting, and charging. (General Management Practices) [General Management Practices]

2. D - The Access Management Process is an activity within the Information Security Management Practice. (General Management Practices) [General Management Practices]

3. D - The goals of Service Portfolio Management are to realize and create maximum value, while minimizing risks and costs. (General Management Practices) [General Management Practices]

4. B - Tools and databases can be used to capture Data, Information, and Knowledge, while Wisdom is a concept relating to abilities to use knowledge to make correct judgments and decisions. (General Management Practices) [General Management Practices]

5. A - The Knowledge Management Practice is introduced in the General Management Category of Practices. (General Management Practices) [General Management Practices]

6. C - The main challenge in the implementation of Information Security Management is to ensure adequate support of company business security and senior management. If this is missing, it is impossible to establish an effective security practice. (General Management Practices) [General Management Practices]

7. D - Information Security Management focuses on the type and extent of data accessible to a user, identify of a user, and the rights of a user. (General Management Practices) [General Management Practices]

8. C - Organizational service investments are divided into 3 categories. Transform the business (TTB), where investments move the organization into new market areas. Grow the business, where investments (GTB) enable an organization to increase the scope of its service offerings. Run the business (RTB), where investments are intended to maintain the current service offerings. (General Management Practices) [General Management Practices]

9. C - Information Security Management ensures that the confidentiality,

integrity, and availability of an organization's assets are maintained. (General Management Practices) [General Management Practices]

10. D - Portfolio Management uses a holistic approach to ensure IT services supporting business processes and services that have been identified as critical are prioritized over less important IT services. (General Management Practices) [General Management Practices]

ITIL Foundation Mock Exam (LITE) - 2

Test Name: ITIL Foundation Mock Exam (LITE) - 2
Total Questions: 40
Correct Answers Needed to Pass: 30 (75.00%)
Time Allowed: 60 Minutes

Test Description

This is the second cumulative ITIL Foundation test which can be used as an indicator for overall performance. This practice test includes questions from all ITIL categories.

Test Questions

1. As his company continues to grow, Kyle is experiencing difficulty keeping track of the various suppliers he is dealing with on a day-to-day basis. He is considering hiring a _____ to handle performance management of the suppliers.

   A. Supplier Manager

   B. IT Asset Manager

   C. Project Manager

   D. Service Integrator

2. What is a RACI model used for?

   A. Performance analysis

   B. Monitoring services

   C. Recording configuration items

   D. Defining roles and responsibilities

3. _____ is a repeatable model of dealing with a particular Category of Change.

   A. Change Model

   B. Change Control

   C. Change Management

   D. A Standard Change

4. Karl's Rentals main business is leasing automobiles. However, he also provides various offerings to address other travel needs including insurance, complimentary bottled water, and baby seats. Combined with car rentals, these "extras" can be referred to as "service _____".

A. Service Offerings

B. Specials

C. Service Promotions

D. Service Provisions

5. David is the IT Director at Miracle Industries and is negotiating a Service Level Agreements with Allied Technologies to provide laptops for the new warehouse employees. Which activity of the SVC does this fall into?

A. Deliver/Support

B. Design & Transition

C. Obtain/Build

D. Engage

6. Which of the following is an example of a Configuration Item?

A. Server configurations

B. RFCs

C. SLAs

D. All of the above

7. Test plans, deployment plans, schedule, and budget are part of which of the following items?

A. Service Strategy

B. Service Design Package

C. Service Catalog

D. Definitive media library

8. To whom does a service in ITIL provide value? I) Customer; II) Service provider; III) IT; IV) General public

A. Customer, Service Provider and IT

B. Customer, Service Provider, IT and general public

C. Service Provider and IT

D. Customer and Service Provider

9. Which of the following statements are TRUE with respect to Configuration items? I) CIs may be grouped and managed together. II) CIs should be selected, classified and identified so that they are traceable throughout their lifecycle. III) CIs may vary largely in complexity, size and type. IV) CIs

can be a piece of hardware or a module of software.

A. All of them

B. I, III and IV

C. I, II and III

D. II, III and IV

10. The Continual Service Improvement Practice consists of:

A. Designing, developing, and implementing service management as a strategic resource.

B. Achieving effectiveness and efficiency in providing and supporting services in order to ensure value for the customer and the service provider.

C. Creating and maintaining customer value through design improvement, service introduction, and operation

D. Developing appropriate IT services, including architecture, processes, policy, and documents.

11. What questions should an organization answer while developing a service strategy?

A. What capabilities and capacities will we require?

B. What products and services will we offer?

C. What is the current strategy?

D. All of the above

12. Stu from New Business Development has signed a contract to provide technical support for new corporate partner. He needs to source 50 new workstations and contacts Jose, the manager of _____ _____ Practice.

A. IT Asset Management

B. Supplier Management

C. Availability Management

D. Portfolio Management

13. The IT Steering Committee is planning to implement a new initiative to improve customer satisfaction. In order to tract these improvements and establish progress towards their goals,

they must establish a/an _____ from which to measure success.

A. Deadline

B. Baseline

C. Objective

D. Assessment

14. Predicting and balancing capabilities, resources, and demand are the goals of which of the following processes?

A. Service Configuration Management

B. Service Configuration Management

C. Capacity and Performance Management

D. IT Asset Management

15. Which of the following is a type of chart used to help monitor and report on Service Level Agreement achievement levels?

A. SLAM

B. SDLC

C. SWOT

D. SWAG

16. Fran is the Human Resources Manager at Saddleback Industries. Realizing that _____ _____ is everyone's responsibility, she established a one hour training session during new employee orientation dedicated to this ideology.

A. Continual Improvement

B. Change Control

C. Portfolio Management

D. Training

17. Events are classified by three thresholds: Informational, Warning and _____.

A. Exception

B. Problem

C. Known Error

D. Incident

18. "Simplicity is the best route to achieving quick wins" is the mantra of the "_____" Guiding Principle.

   A. Keep It Simple and Practical

   B. Start Where You Are

   C. Optimize and Automate

   D. Progress Iteratively with Feedback

19. Ernesto owns a small travel agency. He prides himself on providing a travel experience tailored to each individual traveler. He has adopted a concept known as _____.

   A. Customer Service

   B. Customer Support

   C. Client Management

   D. Service Management

20. Which of the following ITIL Practices covers topics which include the development of internal and external markets, service assets and the service catalog?

   A. Service Design

   B. Continual Improvement

   C. Change Control

   D. Strategy Management

21. A scheme developed to manage suppliers can be defined as _____.

   A. Supplier Categorization

   B. Supplier Management

   C. IT Asset Management

   D. Service Integration

22. Which of the statements below are true? a. Both Resources and Capabilities are types of assets b. Capabilities are easier for an organization to acquire than Resources

   A. B

   B. Both statements are false

   C. A

   D. A and B

23. A customer information database is guaranteed to be available Monday-Friday, 8:00 AM - 5:00 PM. What is this guarantee called?

A. Utility

B. Value

C. Underpinning Contract

D. Warranty

24. A technique used to take the output from one part of a process and used as input to the same process is called a _____ _____.

A. Feedback Loop

B. Continual Improvement

C. ROI

D. PDCA

25. Which of the following statements is NOT an example of an Incident?

A. A user submits a Service Desk call stating he is not able to open an application after an upgrade.

B. A user calls the Service Desk to log a request to configure a new printer.

C. A user logs a call to Service Desk stating his emails to the external domains are bouncing.

D. A user logs a call stating his inability to print.

26. Which one of the following is the primary goal of the Portfolio Management Practice?

A. To support the Service Management Practice by managing information storage and access.

B. To articulate the business needs and the provider's response to those needs.

C. To articulate the IT support needs and the Portfolio Management Practice.

D. To manage the suppliers and their services which in turn help the provider to run his services with an ultimate goal of value for money.

27. What role is responsible for ensuring IT recovery plans are up to date and would be a key resource in the event of a fail-over to a secondary location following a disaster scenario?

A. Availability Manager

B. IT Service Continuity Manager

C. Security Manager

D. Capacity Manager

28. Which of the statements below are true about the ITIL concept of Good Practice? a. Good Practice represents Best Practices which have been commonly accepted and applied throughout the industry   b. Good Practice is often referred to as the most appropriate and is considered to be complete, with no gaps   c. Good Practice reflects an approach to an undertaking which has not yet been proven to be successful

A. A

B. C

C. A and B

D. All of these responses / All of the above

29. Which type of SLA offers the most flexibility and efficiency for an organization?

A. Service-based

B. Customer-based

C. Multi-level

D. Underpinning Contract

30. Which of the following activities is not part of the Strategy Management Practice?

A. Preparation for implementation

B. Development of strategic assets

C. Development of the offer

D. Value net configuration

31. Which of the following is NOT an ITIL Practice?

A. Supplier management

B. Capacity and Performance management

C. Service Catalog management

D. Process management

ITIL Foundation Mock Exam (LITE) 2 - Practice Questions

32. Jeanie uses her company's internet connection to do the research required for her job as a marketing manager. In this scenario, Jeanie is the:

   A. Client

   B. Customer

   C. Internal customer

   D. User

33. A roll back plan and Remediation criteria are decision support tools developed during the _____ planning.

   A. Service Desk

   B. Early Life Support

   C. Change Control

   D. Service Delivery

34. What data point would be used as a starting point to measure the effect of a Service Improvement Plan?

   A. Service Analysis

   B. Capacity Analysis

   C. Baseline

   D. Configuration Database Entry

35. The South Seas Shipping IT division supports 17 business offices around the globe. The services offered and managed by the IT division, as well as the Value Proposition and business cases for the services are captured in what repository?

   A. Portfolio

   B. Service Description

   C. Service Package

   D. Service Catalog

36. Which dimension of a service covers roles and responsibilities, formal organizational structures, culture and staffing requirements?

   A. Communication systems and knowledge bases

   B. Workflow management and inventory systems

   C. Organization and People

D. Roles and responsibilities

37. Which of the following statements are FALSE with respect to the IT Service Industry: I) Whenever a new service is conceived and launched, all the activities ensure that business value is retained and it produces results as expected II) When a new service is introduced, there are always ways to look at it in the form of improvement opportunities. III) The Continual Improvement practice provides feedback only to the Strategy Management Practice.

A. I

B. III

C. All of these statements are false

D. II

38. What is a common method for prioritizing an Incident in ITIL?

A. Prioritize the Incident based on the user's position within the organization.

B. Prioritize the Incident based on First-Come-First-Serve basis.

C. Prioritize the Incident based on the Impact and Urgency of the effect on the customers

D. Allow the Incident to follow the normal route of action and escalation and closure.

39. What item is recorded in the SLA, and defines the expected times for which a customer should have access to a particular service?

A. Demand

B. Capacity

C. Utility

D. Availability

40. Which of the following statement(s) are TRUE with respect to the IT Service Industry? I) Over a period of time all services, including the newly designed ones, undergo changes and improvements. II) As business and business needs change, business outcomes also change. III) To improve the service and service quality, investment is always sought after in new technologies IV) Information should always be recorded as events, incidents or problems

A. I, II and IV

B. I, II and III

C. II, III and IV

D. None of these statements are true

ITIL Foundation Mock Exam (LITE) - 2
Answer Key and Explanations

1. D - A Service Integrator focuses on providing end-to-end service or "Service Integration and Management" (SIAM) and can be an internal role or provisioned from outside the enterprise. (Generic Concepts and Definitions) [General Management Practices]

2. D - The RACI matrix is used to define responsibility and accountability. RACI stands for responsible, accountable, consulted, informed. (Generic Concepts and Definitions) [Generic Concepts and Definitions]

3. A - A Change Model includes specific pre-defined steps that will be followed for a Change of this Category. (Service Management Practice) [Service Management Practices]

4. A - Benefits offered to add value to the original services, generally for an additional fee, are referred to as Service Offerings. (Service Management Practices) [Service Management Practices]

5. D - David is currently in the Engage activity of negotiating the terms of the purchase transaction. (SVC) [SVC - Service Value Chain]

6. D - A Configuration Item is any component that supports an IT service, including IT components, RFCs, Incident Records, and SLAs. (Service Management Practices) [Service Management Practices]

7. B - A Service Design Package (SDP) contains the requirements and relevant design/ build/ deploy/ support information for a new service. A new SDP is created for every new service, as well as when a service has major changes or is retired. (Service Management Practices) [Service Management Practices]

8. A - Services in ITIL provides value to the Customer, Service Provider and IT. (ITIL Concepts) [ITIL Concepts]

9. A - All the statements are TRUE with respect to Configuration items. I) CIs may be grouped and managed together II) CIs should be selected, classified and identified so that they are traceable throughout the lifecycle. III) CIs may vary largely in complexity, size and type. IV) CIs can be a piece of hardware or a module of software. (ITIL Concepts) [ITIL Concepts]

10. C - Continual Improvement is the phase of creating and maintaining

customer value through design improvement, service introduction, and operation. (General Management Practices) [General Management Practices]

11. D - One goal of a service strategy is to identify the competition and to compete with them by distinguishing oneself from the rest and by delivering superior performances. (ITIL Concepts) [ITIL Concepts]

12. B - As the manager of Supplier Management, Jose can work with the corporate suppliers to negotiate the best contract for these resources. (General Management Practices) [General Management Practices]

13. B - There is a need to establish a starting point or Baseline from which improvements (or not) can be periodically measured and reported to stakeholders. (General Management Practices) [General Management Practices]

14. C - Capacity and Performance Management provides predictive capacity indicators, and balances resources, capabilities, and demand. (Service Management Practices) [Service Management Practices]

15. A - A Service Level Achievement Monitoring (SLAM) chart is typically color coded to show whether each agreed Service Level Target has been met, missed, or nearly missed during each of the previous monitoring period. (Service Management Practices) [Service Management Practices]

16. A - Continual Improvement is everyone's responsibility. Establishing this ideology during the first days of employment is one way to encourage its practice. (General Concepts and Definitions) [Generic Concepts and Definitions]

17. A - They are Informational, Warning and Exception. Exception status can cause a degradation to a service. (ITIL Concepts) [ITIL Concepts]

18. A - The "Keep it Simple and Practical" Principle dictates using the minimum action necessary. Always look at the projected outcome of an action before taking that step. (ITIL Concepts) [ITIL Concepts]

19. D - Ernesto has adopted a concept known as Service Management. (Service Management Practices) [Service Management Practices]

20. D - Strategy Management covers topics which include the development of internal and external markets, service assets and the service catalog.

(General Management Practices) [General Management Practices]

21. A - Supplier Categorization is a scheme developed to manage different types of suppliers. (General Management Practices) [General Management Practices]

22. C - Resources are easier for an organization to acquire than Capabilities. Capabilities relate to the specific management, processes, and knowledge within the organization. (General Management Practices) [General Management Practices]

23. D - Warranty is the assurance that a service will meet specific requirements for availability, capacity, and reliability. A warranty is sometimes anchored with a formal agreement such as a Service Level Agreement. (ITIL Concepts) [ITIL Concepts]

24. A - A Feedback Loop is a technique used to take the output from one part of a process and used as input to the same process. (Generic Concepts and Definitions) [Generic Concepts and Definitions]

25. B - A user calls Service Desk to log a request to configure a new printer. This is a Service Request and not an Incident. (Service Management Practices) [Service Management Practices]

26. B - The primary goal of the Portfolio Management Practice is to articulate business needs and the provider's response to those needs. (General Management Practices) [General Management Practices]

27. B - The IT Service Continuity Manager performs the activities above, and also develops and maintains a Service Continuity Plan. (Service Management Practices) [Service Management Practices]

28. C - Good Practice has already evolved from Best Practice, and is considered to be proven and successful. (ITIL Concepts) [ITIL Concepts]

29. C - Multi-level SLAs permit an organization to customize services and service offerings, while minimizing the effort required to do so. (Service Management Practices) [Service Management Practices]

30. D - The four most important activities of the Strategy Management Practice are defining the market, development of the offer, development of strategic assets, and preparation for implementation. (General Management Practices) [General Management Practices]

31. D - Process Management is not an ITIL Practice in V4. (ITIL Concepts) [ITIL Concepts]

32. D - Jeanie is a user in this scenario. ITIL defines a customer as a person that negotiates for and procures IT services, whereas a user is a person who uses an IT service on a daily basis. (ITIL Concepts) [ITIL Concepts]

33. C - The Change Control Practice develops systems and processes for knowledge transfer as necessary for an effective delivery of the service, and to make organization and support decision-making possible. (Service Management Practices) [Service Management Practices]

34. C - A baseline is a benchmark used as a reference point, such as the start of a cycle of Change, used to measure the effect or performance of that Change. (ITIL Concepts) [ITIL Concepts]

35. A - A Portfolio describes a provider's services in terms of business value. They include the complete set of services managed by a service provider, as well as supporting data such as requirements, Value Proposition, risks, and costs. (ITIL Concepts) [ITIL Concepts]

36. C - The Organizations and People Dimension of a service covers roles and responsibilities, formal organization structures, culture and staffing requirements. (ITIL Concepts) [ITIL Concepts]

37. B - The Continual Improvement Practice provides feedback to every other ITIL Practice. (Service Management Practices) [Service Management Practices]

38. C - In ITIL, an Incident is prioritized based on the Impact and Urgency of the effect of the Incident on production. This is called prioritizing an Incident. (Service Management Practices) [Service Management Practices]

39. D - Availability defines when a customer should expect to have access to a particular service and is defined in the SLA. (Service Management Practices) [Service Management Practices]

40. B - The following statements are TRUE with respect to the IT Service Industry: I) Over a period of time all services including the newly designed ones undergo changes and improvements II) As business and business needs change, business outcomes also change III) To improve the service and service quality,

investment is always sought after in new technologies (Service Management Practices) [Service Management Practices]

Knowledge Area Quiz: Generic Concepts and Definitions

Test Name: Knowledge Area Quiz: Generic Concepts and Definitions
Total Questions: 10
Correct Answers Needed to Pass: 7 (70.00%)
Time Allowed: 10 Minutes

Test Description

This practice test targets the Generic Concepts and Definitions of ITIL.

Test Questions

1. What term best reflects a temporary method of resolving an issue, difficulty, or service interruption?

   (A.) Workaround

   B. Incident

   C. Known Error

   D. Service Request

2. Applying context to data results in which of the following?

   A. Wisdom

   B. Knowledge

   (C.) Information

   D. Facts

3. The network engineering team at Atlantis Communications is comparing results of tests conducted on a network that has been recently upgraded to what are considered to be the standard performance levels. This new performance level now becomes the _____ for future comparison.

   A. Service Level

   (B.) Baseline

   C. Performance Report

   D. Change Point

✝4. Fill in the blank: A _____ is a specified way to carry out an activity.

   (A.) Process

   B. Task

   C. Operating instruction

Knowledge Area Quiz: Generic Concepts and Definitions - Practice Questions

D. Procedure

5. Lynn has established CSFs and KPIs for Acme Enterprises utilizing the _____ principle.

   A. Target

   B. RACI

   C. Stakeholder

   D. SMART

6. Patrick is considering adding to his service offerings but wants to identify these services offerings and verify the customers perspective of their _____. Patrick needs to know why the consumer uses the services, what these services help them reach their goals and any risks involved for either party.

   A. Use

   B. Value

   C. Cost

   D. A Product

7. What concept/tool allows management to better understand a service's quality requirements, and presents both the associated costs and expected benefits?

   A. Technical Service Catalogue

   B. Business Case

   C. Service Portfolio

   D. Risk Analysis

8. The average time within which a Configuration Item is brought back up after a failure is called:

   A. Restore Point Objective

   B. Service Recovery Objective

   C. Mean Time to Restore Service

   D. Mean Time Between Failures

9. Critical business processes are identified during which activity?

   A. Vulnerability Assessment

   B. Business Impact Analysis

   C. Risk Assessment

Knowledge Area Quiz: Generic Concepts and Definitions - Practice Questions

D. Threat Assessment

10. Which of the following statements best describes the relationship between procedures and work instructions?

A. A work instruction may include activities and stages from different processes, while a procedure only focuses on a single activity within a work instruction.

B. A procedure describes who should carry out logically related activities, while work instructions define how activities in a procedure should be carried out at a highly detailed level.

C. A work instruction describes who should carry out logically related activities, while procedures define how activities in a work instruction should be carried out.

D. A work instruction only focuses on who must complete a given unit of work, while a procedure only focuses on how the work will be performed.

Knowledge Area Quiz: Generic Concepts and Definitions Answer Key and Explanations

1. A - A Workaround provides a temporary means of resolving an issue for which an underlying root cause has not yet been resolved. (Generic Concepts and Definitions) [Generic Concepts and Definitions]

2. C - Information is derived from applying context, or meaning, to data. (Generic Concepts and Definitions) [Generic Concepts and Definitions]

3. B - A baseline is a benchmark used as a reference for later comparison. (Generic Concepts and Definitions) [Generic Concepts and Definitions]

4. D - A procedure is a specified way to carry out an activity or a process. It describes the how and can also describe who carries out the activity. A procedure may include stages from different processes. A work instruction also describes the steps needed to carry out an activity, but at a much greater level of detail. (Generic Concepts and Definitions) [Generic Concepts and Definitions]

5. D - Utilizing the specific, measurable, achievable, relevant and time-bound (SMART) principle, Lynn was able to define the journey to the exact destination of their improvement project. (Generic Concepts and Definitions). [Generic Concepts and Definitions]

6. B - Patrick is verifying the value of the new services by performing a brief survey of his current customer base. (Generic Concepts and Definitions) [Generic Concepts and Definitions]

7. B - A Business Case presents management with a service's quality requirements and associated delivery costs, in addition to models which outline what a service is expected to achieve. (Generic Concepts and Definitions) [Generic Concepts and Definitions]

8. C - The Mean Time to Restore Service (MTRS) is the time within which a service is back up after a failure. (Generic Concepts and Definitions) [Generic Concepts and Definitions]

9. B - A Business Impact Analysis (BIA) identifies critical business processes, as well as the possible damage or loss caused by disruption to those processes. (Generic Concepts and Definitions) [Generic Concepts and Definitions]

10. B - A procedure describes who should carry out logically related activities,

while work instructions define how activities in a procedure should be carried out at a highly detailed level. (Generic Concepts and Definitions) [Generic Concepts and Definitions]

ITIL Foundation Mock Exam (LITE) - 3

Test Name: ITIL Foundation Mock Exam (LITE) - 3
Total Questions: 40
Correct Answers Needed to Pass: 30 (75.00%)
Time Allowed: 60 Minutes

Test Description

This is the third cumulative ITIL Foundation test which can be used as an indicator for overall performance. This practice test includes questions from all ITIL areas.

Test Description:

1. Florida Freight and Trucking is conducting a review of its operations to identify Vital Business Functions, underlying dependencies, and recovery objectives. What is this activity called?

   A. Restore point objectives

   B. Business impact analysis

   C. Risk management

   D. Risk analysis

2. ITIL is concerned with which three types of SLAs?

   A. Service-based, Customer-based, and Multilevel

   B. Transaction-level, Reporting-level, Availability-level

   C. Promotional, Permanent, Interim

   D. Corporate-level, Customer-level, and Service-level

3. What role is responsible for formally authorizing changes, and may delegate this responsibility to another role based on pre-defined parameters such as risk and cost?

   A. Change Control Manager

   B. Change Advisory Board

   C. Change Authority

   D. Product Manager

4. Lynne is the CIO an is heading up the Continual Improvement initiative at Acme Enterprises. She wants to establish a gap analysis to report the progress of the initiative. Two

measurements that provide input into this calculation are _____ _____ _____ and ___ _____ _____.

A. Measurement and Reporting

B. Continual Improvement

C. CIR

D. Critical Success Factors (CSFs) and Key Performance Indicators (KPIs)

5. A new operating system platform has been implemented at Lincoln Utilities during the weekend change window. However, it has been discovered that the new platform is affecting the availability of the organization's billing system. Which of the following will be implemented to address this?

   A. Change control

   B. Remediation plan

   C. Rollback plan

   D. Patch management

6. Assessment of costs, capabilities, and demand is part of which ITIL Practice?

   A. Service Financial Management

   B. Budgeting

   C. Demand Management

   D. Portfolio Management

7. Dan is the Availability Manager of Mid-West Telecom. What level of availability is he responsible for achieving?

   A. Availability that meets or exceeds the business requirements.

   B. 99.99%

   C. 99.50%

   D. 100%

8. During a client discussion, you are asked to summarize the meaning of an Incident. Which of the items below most appropriately defines an Incident?

   A. A disruption for which the root cause is known

   B. A support request not involving a failure in the IT infrastructure

   C. The unknown root cause of one or more disruptions to Service

ITIL Foundation Mock Exam (LITE) 3 - Practice Questions

D. Any event which may lead to the disruption, or decreased quality, of a Service

9. The entry to Incident Management Practice can come from which of the following? I) Events communicated directly by users II) Through Service Desk III) Through tools used for Event Management IV) Through hardware resources

   A. II and IV

   B. I, II and III

   C. only II

   D. I and III

10. Using a tool to monitor the behavior of enterprise applications and manage these applications to keep services available at all times is an example of what ITIL Practice?

    A. Service Support

    B. Monitoring and Event Control

    C. Service Management

    D. Plan, Do, Check, Act

11. In order to predict future demand for the service that he manages, Ted is reviewing the processes and activities of the sales department over time. He has discovered that activity levels typically increase at month-, quarter-, and year-end. What is this set of metrics he is reviewing called?

    A. Service Level Agreements

    B. Patterns of Business Activities

    C. Availability reports

    D. Capacity reports

12. Which Capacity Management subprocess focuses on the performance and utilization of disk, CPU, and memory utilization in a server?

    A. Service capacity management

    B. Service operation agreement

    C. Onsite Service Agreement

    D. Service Performance and Capacity Analysis and Service Performance and Capacity Planning include the utilization of resources.

13. Which approach to Pre-Program ROI is the best choice?

    A. Internal Rate of Return

    B. Net Present Value

    C. Accrual Accounting

    D. Cashflow Basis

14. A service enables value co-creation by facilitating _____ customers want to achieve.

    A. Objectives

    B. Outcomes

    C. Outputs

    D. Results

15. TechCo, an IT service provider, is known for being a market leader in the field of complex system development. Which of the following items would not be considered an asset which TechCo possesses?

    A. Capital

    B. Value

    C. Infrastructure

    D. Knowledge

16. Which practices are typically involved in the implementation of a problem resolution: 1) Continual improvement; 2) Service request management; 3) Service level management; 4) Change control

    A. 1 & 4

    B. 2 & 3

    C. 1 & 2

    D. 3 & 4

17. Connecting Point Software and Diatomic Systems have arranged to host each other's IT infrastructure in the event either of them experiences a disaster that affects their mission critical applications. What is this type of disaster recovery measure called?

    A. Quid pro quo

    B. Gradual Recovery

    C. Disaster Planning

    D. Reciprocal Arrangement

18. ITIL defines 3 types of change requests. Which of the following is not one of these types?

   A. Strategic

   B. Standard

   C. Normal

   D. Emergency

19. During which Category of ITIL Practices are IT budgets set?

   A. Service Design

   B. Technical Management Practices

   C. Service Management Practices

   D. General Management Practices

20. What ITIL Practice manages the source of information on all practices offered in the pipeline, catalog and those retired?

   A. Portfolio Management

   B. Service Design

   C. Service Catalog Management

   D. Service Configuration Management

21. Which Category of the ITIL Practices contains the Service Design Practice?

   A. Technical Management Practices

   B. Service Design

   C. General Management Practices

   D. Service Management Practices

22. What role is responsible for identifying and documenting the value of services within an organization and provides cost information to Portfolio Management?

   A. Product Manager

   B. Demand Manager

   C. Service Financial Manager

   D. Service Level Manager

23. Which of the following is not included in the Service Management Category of ITIL Practices?

   A. Service Desk

ITIL Foundation Mock Exam (LITE) 3 - Practice Questions

B. Monitoring and Event Reporting

C. Deployment Management

D. Service Continuity Management

24. A fire in the datacenter that takes out several mission critical systems and leaves the company unable to conduct key business work is an example of what type of Incident?

A. Managed Incident

B. Catastrophic Incident

C. Emergency Incident

D. Major Incident

25. Which of the following is a valid response to an event?

A. Event logging

B. Creation of an RFC

C. Human interaction

D. All of these responses / All of the above

26. Services are delivered to internal and external service consumers through the coordination and integration of the _____ of Service Management.

A. SVC

B. Value Proposition

C. Guiding Principles

D. Four Dimensions of Service Management

27. Under Service Configuration Management in ITIL, this system holds information on all of an organization's Configuration Items (CIs).

A. Service Configuration Management System

B. Configuration Item (CI)

C. Service Catalogue

D. Service Knowledge Management System (SKMS)

28. The shared services group at Global Storage Technology has developed a service catalog that contains the IT Services, processes, supporting services, and components offered to its customers. This catalog, however,

ITIL Foundation Mock Exam (LITE) 3 - Practice Questions

is not intended to be viewed by the customer. What is this catalog called?

A. Technical Service Catalog

B. Business Service Catalog

C. Configuration Management Catalog

D. Operation Catalog

29. Which of the statements below can be considered true / correct? a. The Service Desk should act as the main source of information for users, and should provide users with information regarding current and expected errors. b. The Service Desk should be capable of providing users with information regarding SLA provisions, new and existing services, and order procedures.

A. B

B. A

C. None of the above

D. All of these responses / All of the above

30. Which one of the following statements do NOT form an output from Service V model of the Service Validation and Testing Process?

A. Test plan and design.

B. Testing environment details and the configuration baselines.

C. Test models and test activity details.

D. Test results and Analysis of test results.

31. _____ is everyone's responsibility.

A. Availability

B. Service

C. Delivery

D. Continual improvement

32. Availability, capacity, and continuity are attributes of which of the following?

A. Utility

B. Warranty

C. Demand Management

D. Portfolio Management

33. A large law firm is evaluating a new email service offered by a managed service provider. The law firm is determining if the service meets a specific functional requirement. The ability of the email service to do so is best described by which of the following terms?

   A. Value

   B. Utility

   C. Capacity

   D. Warranty

34. Jennifer is an engineer director at a managed hosting company. She is in charge of the processes by which new patches will be deployed, and works with other engineers to design the most effective mechanisms for the patching efforts. In what role is Jennifer acting?

   A. Process Owner

   B. Management representative

   C. Service Owner

   D. Service Deployment

35. Under Continual Improvement, an established starting data point used to for comparison in the future is known as what?

   A. Metric

   B. Baseline

   C. Validation

   D. Event

36. During which ITIL Practice are suppliers categorized in the Supplier and Contract Database?

   A. Supplier Management

   B. IT Asset Management

   C. Continual Improvement

   D. Service Management Practices

37. High Seas Semiconductor has a very mature shared services IT group that services the IT needs of all the organizations' locations and subsidiaries around the world. What is the term for the aggregation of data and tools that High Seas uses to manage the full lifecycle of its services?

A. Service Configuration Database

B. Configuration Management Database

C. Service Catalog

D. Configuration Management System

38. In an effort to eliminate wasted resources, the second Guiding Principle is _____.

A. Improve

B. Value Streams & processes

C. Plan

D. Start where you are

39. The management team at a large data center has just been informed by their telecommunications provider that a fiber cable cut has caused a regional outage that will not be repaired for at least 12 hours. This duration exceeds the SLAs for the data center, and the management team has notified the executive management team of this situation. The executive management team issues communications to affected business units regarding the situation and the potential duration of the outage. What is this type of escalation called?

A. Hierarchical Escalation

B. Priority Escalation

C. 4th Tier

D. Functional Escalation

40. Which of the following terms refers to the ability of a service or component to perform as intended over a specific duration of time?

A. Availability

B. Resilience

C. Serviceability

D. Reliability

ITIL Foundation
Mock Exam (LITE) - 3
Answer Key and Explanations

1. B - During Business Impact Analysis an organization identifies the functions that are absolutely critical to the success of the organization, the underlying services, infrastructure, and other dependencies required to support them, and how quickly and to what extent these functions must be brought back online in the event of an outage. (Generic Concepts and Definitions) [Generic Concepts and Definitions]

2. A - Three types of SLA structures discussed within ITIL are Service-based, Customer-based, and Multilevel. (Service Management Practices) [Service Management Practices]

3. C - The Change Authority (which is a given role, person, or group) is responsible for the activities listed above. (Service Management Practices) [Service Management Practices]

4. D - Critical Success Factors (CSFs) and Key Performance Indicators (KPIs) are two measurements that indicate the level of success of an improvement initiative at Acme Enterprises. (Generic Concepts and Definitions) [Generic Concepts and Definitions]

5. B - The Remediation Plan will be implemented to address the service availability with the operating system change. Remediation plans are developed prior to implementation of a change, and may include options, processes, and trigger points to indicate how a malfunctioning change will be dealt with. (Service Management Practices) [Service Management Practices]

6. A - The goal of the Service Financial Management Practice is to clearly define for an organization the costs of providing new and existing services. This practice helps create a balance between opportunities and capabilities. (General Management Practices) [General Management Practices]

7. A - The Availability Manager does not seek to achieve 100% availability, but instead seeks to deliver availability that matches or exceeds the business requirements. (Service Management Practices) [Service Management Practices]

8. D - A support request not resulting from a failure in the IT infrastructure is a type of event (Service Request), but does not cause a degradation in service. (Service Management

Practices) [Service Management Practices]

9. B - The entry to the Incident Management Practice can come from Events communicated directly by users, through Service Desk and through tools used for Monitoring and Event Management. (Service Management Practices) [Service Management Practices]

10. B - Service monitoring and control is based on a continual cycle of monitoring, reporting, and undertaking action. This cycle is crucial to providing, supporting, and improving services. (Service Management Practices) [Service Management Practices]

11. B - Business processes are the primary source of demand for IT services. Analysis of the Patterns of Business Activity allows a service provider to predict, strategically plan for, and respond to changes in demand for supporting services. (ITIL Concepts) [ITIL Concepts]

12. D - Service Performance and Capacity Analysis and Service Performance and Capacity Planning. (Service Management Practices) [Service Management Practices]

13. B - Net Present Value is based on the comparison between cash inflows and cash outflows, where the difference, the "net present value", determines whether or not the investment is valuable. Net Present Value makes a more realistic assumption for the rate of return. (Generic Concepts and Definitions) [Generic Concepts and Definitions]

14. B - The value of a service enables value co-creation by facilitating outcomes that customers want to achieve. (ITIL Concepts) [ITIL Concepts]

15. B - Knowledge, capital, and infrastructure are all types of service assets which contribute to the basis of "value" for a service. (ITIL Concepts) [ITIL Concepts]

16. A - 1) Problem management activities can identify improvement opportunities in all four dimensions of service management. 4) Error control includes identification of potential permanent solutions which may result in a change request for implementation of a solution. (Service Management Practices) [Service Management Practices]

17. D - A reciprocal arrangement is an agreement between two similar sized organizations or businesses to share

disaster recovery obligations. (Service Management Practices) [Service Management Practices]

18. A - There are three types of change requests: normal, standard, and emergency. Strategic change requests are not defined as a change type by ITIL. (ITIL Concepts) [ITIL Concepts]

19. D - IT budgets are set as part of the Service Financial Management Practice in the General Management Practice Category. (General Management Practices) [General Management Practices]

20. A - The Portfolio documents the lifecycle of technology and service CIs in the enterprise. (General Management Practices) [General Management Practices]

21. D - The Service Design Practices are part of the Service Management Practices Category. (Service Management Practices) [Service Management Practices]

22. C - The Service Financial Manager is responsible for identifying and documenting the value of services within an organization and provides cost information to Portfolio Management. (General Management Practices) [General Management Practices]

23. C - Service Desk, Monitoring and Event Management, and Service Continuity Management are Service Management Practices. Deployment Management is a Technical Management Practice. (Technical Management Practices) [Technical Management Practices]

24. D - A Major Incident is the highest category of impact for an Incident. A Major Incident results in significant disruption to the business. (ITIL Concepts) [ITIL Concepts]

25. D - The response to an Event can have many forms, and a combination of response forms is possible. (Service Management Practices) [Service Management Practices]

26. D - The Four Dimensions of Service Management delivers services to internal and external service consumers. (ITIL Concepts) [ITIL Concepts]

27. A - Under ITIL, the Service Configuration Management System is the overarching platform holding information on all of an organization's Configuration Items. (Service Management Practices) [Service Management Practices]

28. A - The Technical Service Catalog contains details of all the IT Services delivered to the customer, together with relationships to the supporting services, shared services, components, and Configuration Items necessary to support the provision of the service to the business. This should underpin the Business Service Catalog and not form part of the customer view. (Service Management Practices) [Service Management Practices]

29. D - Both of the statements are true and correct in regard to the Service Desk's duty to provide information to users. (Service Management Practices) [Service Management Practices]

30. A - Test plan and design is not an output from the Service Validation and Testing process. (Service Management Practices) [Service Management Practices]

31. D - It is everyone's responsibility to identify areas for improvement. (Generic Concepts and Definitions) [Generic Concepts and Definitions]

32. B - Warranty of services provides a customer with reassurance and guarantees that a specific service meets the customer's requirements. Availability, capacity, and continuity are some of the service levels on which warranty is based. (Generic Concepts and Definitions) [Generic Concepts and Definitions]

33. B - Utility is the functionality offered by a service to meet a particular need. Utility is often defined as "what the service does." (ITIL Generic Concepts and Definitions) [Generic Concepts and Definitions]

34. A - The Process Owner is responsible for the process strategy, assists in the design, and ensures that all process activities are carried out. (ITIL Concept) [ITIL Concepts]

35. B - A baseline is an initial starting point used to make comparisons against in the future. (Generic Concepts and Definitions) [Generic Concepts and Definitions]

36. A - During the Supplier Management Practice, suppliers required to support an organization's IT services are identified and categorized. (General Management Practices) [General Management Practices]

37. A - The Service Configuration Database is the complete set of tools and databases that are used to manage knowledge and information necessary to make decisions and execute IT Service Management processes.

ITIL Foundation Mock Exam (LITE) 3 - Answer Key and Explanations

(Service Management Practices) [Service Management Practices]

38. D - In an effort to eliminate wasted resources, the second Guiding Principle is "Start where you are" (ITIL Concepts) [ITIL Concepts]

39. A - Hierarchical escalations, also known as vertical escalations, are used when resolution of an Incident will not be within set timeframes or be a satisfactory resolution. (ITIL Concepts) [ITIL Concepts]

40. A - Availability is the ability of an IT service or component to perform its required function at a stated instant or over a stated period of time. (Service Management Practices) [Service Management Practices]

Knowledge Area Quiz: ITIL Concepts

Test Name: Knowledge Area Quiz: ITIL Concepts
Total Questions: 10
Correct Answers Needed to Pass: 7 (70.00%)
Time Allowed: 10 Minutes

Test Description

This practice test focuses on selected ITIL Concepts.

Test Questions

1. Delta Solutions offers a number of specialized organizational capabilities which provide value to their customers in the form of services. What term best reflects these capabilities?

    A. Service Management Practices

    B. ITIL

    C. Encapsulation

    D. Agency Principle

2. Fitness for use, or the availability, reliability, continuity and security, representing a decline in possible losses, is best reflected by what term?

    A. Warranty

    B. Utility

    C. Service

    D. Value

3. Fill in the blank: _____ is where the approved versions of all media CIs are stored and monitored.

    A. Definitive Media Library

    B. CMDB

    C. Definitive spares

    D. Secure library

4. Which of the following statements describing a practice in ITIL are true?
   a. An ITIL Practice includes all of the resources required to deliver the outputs. b. An ITIL Practice may not define or revise organizational policies or standards

    A. Both statements are false

B. A

C. A and B

D. B

5. A large aircraft engineering corporation has created a repository containing information about its shared data integration middleware service. It includes information about all areas of the service, from business and service level requirements to operations plans and acceptance criteria. What is this collective body of information called?

   A. Service Portfolio

   B. Service Design Package

   C. Business Impact Analysis

   D. Service Catalog

6. An escalation based on knowledge or skills is referred to as what?

   A. Tier 2 Escalation

   B. Functional Escalation

   C. Hierarchical Escalation

   D. Engineering Escalation

7. A process is a logically coherent series of activities for a pre-defined goal. What is the Process Owner responsible for?

   A. The result of the process

   B. Setting up the process

   C. Implementing the process

   D. Describing the process

8. A liaison between the finance team requesting additional application functionality and the application's end users is the _____.

   A. Advisor

   B. Supervisor

   C. Business Relationship Manager

   D. Power user

9. Which of the following statements regarding the Portfolio are true? a. The Portfolio should form part of a Service Configuration Management Practice. b. The Portfolio should be documented within an organization's

Service Configuration Management Practice.

A. A

B. A and B

C. B

D. None of the above are true.

10. Which of the following is not a reactive activity?

A. Problem Resolution

B. Monitoring

C. Incident Handling

D. Capacity Planning

Knowledge Area Quiz: ITIL Concepts Answer Key and Explanations

1. A - The term Service Management is most applicable to the specialized organizational capabilities which provide value to customers in the form of services. (ITIL Concepts) [ITIL Concepts]

2. A - Fitness for use describes the concept of "Warranty". (ITIL Concepts) [ITIL Concepts]

3. A - The Definitive Media Library is a secure store where the definitive, authorized versions of all media CIs are stored and monitored. (ITIL Concepts) [ITIL Concepts]

4. B - An ITIL Practice may indeed define and revise organizational policies or standards, as well as guidelines, activities, and work instructions if needed. (ITIL Concepts) [ITIL Concepts]

5. B - A Service Design Package includes all aspects of a service and its requirements, and is used to provide guidance and structure through the entire lifecycle of the service. (ITIL Concepts) [ITIL Concepts]

6. B - Functional Escalations are based on knowledge or expertise, and are also known as Horizontal Escalations. (ITIL Concepts) [ITIL Concepts]

7. A - The Process Owner is responsible for ensuring that the process is implemented as agreed and that the established objectives will therefore be achieved. (ITIL Concepts) [ITIL Concepts]

8. C - Business Relationship Managers are business users who act as liaisons between business and IT. (ITIL Concepts) [ITIL Concepts]

9. B - The Portfolio should be part of an overarching knowledge system and should also be documented in the Service Configuration Management Practice. (ITIL Concepts) [ITIL Concepts]

10. D - Reactive activities are those that revolve around detecting and handling events that have already occurred, and include activities such as monitoring, Problem and Incident Management, and outages. (ITIL Concepts) [ITIL Concepts]

ITIL Foundation Mock Exam (LITE) - 4

Test Name: ITIL Foundation Mock Exam (LITE) - 4
Total Questions: 40
Correct Answers Needed to Pass: 30 (75.00%)
Time Allowed: 60 Minutes

Test Description

This is the fourth cumulative ITIL Foundation test which can be used as an indicator for overall performance. This practice test includes questions from all ITIL areas.

Test Questions

1. Changes are communicated to the employee community by publishing the _____ _____.

   A. Change Schedule

   B. Change Authority

   C. Status Updates

   D. Continuity Schedule

2. Enrique is reviewing the version number of a Configuration Item in the CMDB. The version number is an:

   A. Asset

   B. Attribute

   C. Assembly

   D. Auditable record

3. In what ITIL Practices Category are the majority of Supplier Management process activities performed?

   A. General Management

   B. Service Management Practices

   C. Continual Improvement

   D. Service Design

4. What Service Management Practice must maintain updated and accurate configuration records, in addition to defining and controlling information on the components which make up an organization's services and infrastructure?

   A. Service Configuration Management

B. Measurement and Reporting

C. Change Control

D. Availability Management

5. Widgets International is rolling out a major upgrade to its ERP system. The Service Desk will be manned with extra staff for the first two weeks after the deployment. This is an example of _____.

   A. Service operation

   B. A workaround

   C. Transition planning

   D. Early Life Support

6. Which of the following is NOT a result of a service improvement?

   A. Total Cost of Ownership (TCO)

   B. Return on Investment (ROI)

   C. Value on Investment (VOI)

   D. Service Level Agreement (SLA)

7. The term "service consumer" is a generic role that can identify these specific roles: customers, users and _____.

   A. Creditors

   B. Provider

   C. Sponsors

   D. Supplier

8. A global semiconductor company wants to implement a shared services IT group for the entire organization. They have listed the goals of the project and would like to determine which ITIL Practice groups that should be included to ensure enterprise vision and strategy. What would be one of the best planning tools?

   A. Balanced Score Card

   B. Gap Analysis

   C. Iterative Model

   D. Waterfall Model

9. Which of the items below are valid performance indicators for the Service Desk?   a. Number of incidents resolved without escalation   b. Percentage of incidents properly

logged c. Number of telephone calls which were answered courteously, as reported in customer surveys

A. A and B

B. A and C

C. B and C

D. All of these responses / All of the above

10. Applied heavily under the Continual Improvement Practice, what does the PDCA Model stand for?

A. Produce, Design, Check, Accept

B. Plan, Design, Confirm, Act

C. Produce, Deploy, Change, Accept

D. Plan, Do, Check, Act

11. What role is responsible for the creation and management of demand incentive and penalty schemes, monitors overall demand and capacity, and participates in the creation of SLAs? Delete

A. Service Level Manager

B. Product Manager

C. IT Financial Manager

D. Capacity and Performance Manager

12. To facilitate positive relationships and value for stakeholders is the main goal of the _____ _____ Practice.

A. Relationship Management

B. Continual Improvement

C. Service Configuration Management

D. Supplier Management

13. Configuration Items and the relationships between them are captured in which repository?

A. Relational Database

B. Change Management Database

C. IT Asset Management Database

D. Configuration Management Database

14. Common requests from users for information or changes related to an IT service, such as a password reset, and do not require an RFC is known as what?

A. Service Request

B. Event

C. Problem

D. Alert

15. The Configuration Manager of a state government agency has provided a report on the status of all current and past Configuration Items. What is this activity called?

A. Configuration Accounting

B. Configuration Status

C. Status Accounting

D. Request for Status

16. Which of the following statements are TRUE with respect to the Information Security Management process? I) Business will decide which information is to be classified as confidential and which is to be public II) All business processes except Service Improvement processes should be considered when formulating the level of data protection. III) Information and data protection involve physical and technical aspects.

A. All of the statements are true

B. II and III

C. I and III

D. I and II

17. Which of the following ITIL practices identifies and prioritizes improvement programs according to strategic objectives?

A. Service Design Practice

B. Continual Improvement Practice

C. Availability Management Practice

D. Capacity Management Practice

18. What role is responsible for ensuring agreed levels of service availability are maintained, monitors the actual availability of services achieved, and manages the Availability Plan?

A. Capacity Manager

B. Availability Manager

C. Demand Manager

D. Service Continuity Manager

19. Which of the following are the objectives of Continual Improvement Practices? I) Review and analyze each of the 34 ITIL practices and identify and recommend improvement opportunities II) Review and analyze the results of Service Level achievement III) Keeping customer satisfaction in mind, deliver IT services cost effectively

   A. All of these items are objectives of CSI

   B. II and III only

   C. I and III only

   D. I and II only

20. Which of the following is a downtime measurement of a system or a service?

   A. MTSB

   B. MTBF

   C. MTRS

   D. MTBSI

21. Service Financial Management is comprised of which three activities?

   A. Budgeting, IT accounting, and demand management

   B. Budgeting, IT accounting, and charging

   C. Budgeting, analysis, and charging

   D. Budgeting, opportunity management, and charging.

22. What role is responsible for managing the CMS, as well as for managing the CIs and defining their naming conventions?

   A. Change Manager

   B. Configuration Control Board

   C. Service Asset Manager

   D. Configuration Manager

23. John is the leader of a committee that meets quarterly to determine if the existing IT infrastructure is sufficient

to support current and predicted demand. What is this process called?

A. Business impact analysis

B. Availability planning

C. Capacity planning

D. Demand management

24. Fill in the blank: _____ is an event that interrupts or has the potential to interrupt service.

A. Failure

B. Incident

C. Catastrophe

D. Outage

25. Of the items listed below, where would information relating to an organization's service CIs be stored?

A. KMS

B. CDB

C. CMDB

D. DML

26. The Business Continuity team at Prendergast Manufacturing has begun evaluating its assets, and the threats to and vulnerabilities of these assets. What is this process called?

A. Daily Operational Activity

B. Business Impact Analysis

C. Risk-avoidant behavior

D. Risk Assessment

27. Which of the following is not a technique used when seeking financing for ITIL projects?

A. Value

B. Post-Program ROI

C. Pre-Program ROI

D. Business case

28. A problem with an accounting application has been discovered by the finance team. The application support group has not identified a cause or resolution for this problem, but has devised a way for the finance team to continue working until a permanent resolution is found. This is an example of what type of service response?

A. Event

B. Change

C. Incident

D. Workaround

29. Under ITIL, a process takes one or more _____ and turns them in to defined _____.

A. inputs, outputs

B. stakeholders, customers

C. service assets, customer assets

D. functions, roles

30. Which of the following is not one of the three main types of metrics as defined by Continual Improvement

A. Process

B. Service

C. Supplier Management

D. Technology

31. What statement below best describes the concept of a "Role" in ITIL?

A. A means of delivering value to customers by facilitating outcomes they want to achieve, without the ownership of specific costs and risks.

B. A set of specialized organizational capabilities for providing value to customers in the form of services.

C. A team, unit, or person that performs tasks related to a specific practice or process.

D. A logical concept referring to people and automated measures that execute a defined practice, process, an activity, or a combination thereof.

32. To ensure consistency, professionalism, and efficiency when in contact with the customer, the Service Desk may be provided with set procedures based on questionnaires and standard responses. These standardized procedures, questionnaires and responses used by the Service Desk are collectively known as:

A. Speeches

B. Screenplays

C. Drafts

D. Scripts

33. Which of the following is a model for defining the roles of stakeholders in a process or an activity?

   A. Balanced Score Card

   B. RACI

   C. PDCA

   D. SMART

34. Which General Management Practice is responsible for managing information derived from a number of sources; such as user and support documentation?

   A. Release Management

   B. Change Control

   C. IT Asset and Management

   D. Knowledge Management

35. Which of the statements below are true regarding service assets? a. The performance potential of customer assets increases as service potential is increased   b. Increased customer performance potential results in less demand for the scale or scope of a service.

   A. B

   B. A

   C. Both statements are false

   D. A and B

36. What Service Management Practice focuses on restoring the normal operation of a service as quickly as possible while minimizing any impact to the operation of the business?

   A. Event Management

   B. Problem Management

   C. Change Control

   D. Incident Management

37. What is a consequence of implementing an overly complex practice?

A. Service quality can be lowered if processes are excessively cumbersome.

B. Service quality KPIs will increase.

C. Relevant KPIs become invisible

D. Changes become easier to manage.

38. What Service Management principle focuses on the ability to respond to changes without impacting other services?

A. Stability

B. Quality of Service

C. Responsiveness

D. Cost of Service

39. An organization has outsourced its network design and deployment services to a large integrator. The lessons learned from past design and deployment efforts have led to the development of a plan to improve and enhance the service being offered. Where are these plans recorded?

A. Supplier Quality Reports

B. Supplier Performance Reports

C. Supplier Management Database

D. Business Process Outsourcing

40. Systemix provides managed hosting services. They have a basic hosting package that includes a shared server, 500GB of storage, and domain name registration. Additional services, including static IPs and reporting tools, are available. What are these additional services called?

A. Service Capabilities

B. Service Enhancements

C. Supporting Services

D. Shared Services

ITIL Foundation Mock Exam (LITE) 4 - Practice Questions

ITIL Foundation
Mock Exam (LITE) - 4
Answer Key and Explanations

1. A - The Change Schedule is generally published through the Service Desk and made available to the appropriate personnel. (Service Management Practices) [Service Management Practices]

2. B - An Attribute is a piece of information about a Configuration Item. Examples are name, location, version number, and cost. Attributes of CIs are recorded in the Configuration Management Database. (ITIL Concepts) [ITIL Concepts]

3. A - Supplier Management is strongly rooted within the General Management Category, but some process activities occur in other ITIL Categories. (General Management Practices) [General Management Practices]

4. A - Service Configuration Management is the correct process. (Service Management Practices) [Service Management Practices]

5. D - Early Life Support is intended to offer extra support after the deployment of a new or changed service. (ITIL Concepts) [ITIL Concepts]

6. A - Key benefits / results of service improvements include: * Increased Return on Investment (ROI) * Increased Value on Investment (VOI) In addition, Service Level Agreements (SLAs) must be monitored to ensure service improvement targets are being met. (ITIL Concepts) [ITIL Concepts]

7. C - Service consumers can be defined as a Customer who defines the service requirements; User who actually consume the service; and the Sponsor who pays for the service. (ITIL Concepts) [ITIL Concepts]

8. A - The Balanced Scorecard is a performance management tool for measuring whether the smaller scale operational activities of a company are aligned with its larger scale objectives in terms of vision and strategy. (Generic Concepts and Definitions) [Generic Concepts and Definitions]

9. D - All of the responses are valid performance indicators for the Service Desk. Some performance indicators are more qualitative and best measured via customer surveys, such as whether telephone calls were courteously answered. (Service

Management Practices) [Service Management Practices]

10. D - The PDCA Model, otherwise known as the Deming Cycle, stands for Plan, Do, Check, Act. (Generic Concepts and Definitions) [Generic Concepts and Definitions]

11. D - The Capacity and Performance Manager is responsible for the creation and management of demand incentive and penalty schemes, monitors overall demand and capacity, and participates in the creation of SLAs. (Service Management Practices) [Service Management Practices]

12. A - The goal of Relationship Management is to cultivate positive relationships that provide value for all stakeholders. (Service Management Practices) [Service Management Practices]

13. D - The CMDB is a set of one or more connected databases and information sources that provide a logical model of the IT infrastructure, including CIs and their relationships to each other. (ITIL Concepts) [ITIL Concepts]

14. A - In ITIL, Service Requests are common requests made by users for additional services or for information and do not require a Request for Change (RFC). (Service Management Practices) [Service Management Practices]

15. C - Reporting of all current and historical data for each Configuration Item through its lifecycle is known as Status Accounting. (Service Management Practices) [Service Management Practices]

16. C - The following statements are TRUE with respect to the Information Security management process I) Business will decide which information is to be classified as confidential and which is to be public II) Information and Data protection involves physical and technical aspects. (General Management Practices) [General Management Practices]

17. B - The Continual Improvement Practice identifies learning and improvement opportunities, and prioritizes them in accordance with the organization's strategic objectives. (Service Management Practices) [Service Management Practices]

18. B - The Availability Manager performs the activities above, and also assesses the potential impacts of change in relation to service availability. (Service Management Practices) [Service Management Practices]

ITIL Foundation Mock Exam (LITE) 4 - Answer Key and Explanations

19. D - These are the objectives of the Continual Improvement Practice: I) Review and analyze each of the practices to identify and recommend improvement opportunities II) Review and analyze the results of Service Level achievement. (General Management Practices) [General Management Practices]

20. C - MTRS, or Mean Time to Restore Service, is a measure of the average time a service or system is unavailable after a failure. (ITIL Concepts) [ITIL Concepts]

21. B - Budgeting, IT accounting, and charging are the primary activities performed in Service Financial Management. (General Management Practices) [General Management Practices]

22. D - The Configuration Manager is responsible for managing the Service Configuration Management System, as well as for managing the Configuration Items (CIs) and defining their naming conventions. (Service Management Practices) [Service Management Practices]

23. C - Capacity planning is the process responsible for reviewing, analyzing, and understanding the current load capabilities of a service or its supporting infrastructure, and developing a path forward to ensure that anticipated demand can continue to be met. (Service Management Practices) [Service Management Practices]

24. B - An Incident is any Event that interrupts or can interrupt a service. Events may be reported by customers, the Service Desk, or a tool. (Service Management Practices) [Service Management Practices]

25. C - The Service Management Configuration System would store information on an organization's Service Configuration Items. (Service Management Practices) [Service Management Practices]

26. D - Risk assessment is the evaluation of an organization's assets, threats, and vulnerabilities. (Generic Concepts and Definitions) [Generic Concepts and Definitions]

27. A - Business case, Pre-program ROI, and Post-program ROI are all techniques used when seeking financing for an ITIL project. (Service Management Practices) [Service Management Practices]

28. D - The goal here is to restore normal service operation as quickly as possible to minimize impact on the customer. As such, if Problem

Management can provide a workaround the users can return to production, even though it does not deal with the root cause at that time. (Service Management Practices) [Service Management Practices]

29. A - Under ITIL, a process takes one or more inputs and turns them into defined outputs. (ITIL Concepts) [ITIL Concepts]

30. C - Supplier metrics are defined in the Supplier Management process, not in Continual Improvement. (Service Management Practices) [Service Management Practices]

31. C - ITIL describes a Role as "A team, unit, or person that performs tasks related to a specific practice." (ITIL Concept) [ITIL Concepts]

32. D - Scripts can be provided to the Service Desk in order to provide standardized procedures based on questionnaires and responses, and add to the consistency, efficiency and professionalism of the Service Desk. (Service Management Practices) [Service Management Practices]

33. B - The RACI model helps teams identify who is Responsible, Accountable, Consulted, and Informed. (Generic Concepts and Definitions) [Generic Concepts and Definitions]

34. D - The goal of the Knowledge Management Practice is to enable organizations to improve the quality of management decision making by ensuring that reliable information and data is available throughout the service lifecycle. (General Management Practices) [General Management Practices]

35. B - Increased customer performance potential results in more demand, not less, for the scale or scope of a service. (General Management Practices) [General Management Practices]

36. D - Incident Management focuses on restoring the normal operation of a service as quickly as possible while minimizing any impact to the operation of the business. (Service Management Practices) [Service Management Practices]

37. A - If the Practice procedures become overly complex, the service quality may be adversely affected; unnecessary or over-engineered procedures are seen as bureaucratic obstacles, which are to be avoided where possible. (ITIL Concepts) [ITIL Concepts]

38. C - Responsiveness focuses on the ability to respond to Changes without impacting other services. (Service Management Practices) [Service Management Practices]

39. C - Supplier Service Improvement Plans are used to record all actions and plans agreed between suppliers and service providers and are stored in the Supplier Management Database. (General Management Practices) [General Management Practices]

40. C - A Service Package is made up of the core services provided, additional supporting services that are available, and the service levels. This modular approach allows service providers to avoid one-size-fits all offerings, while still standardizing the services offered. (ITIL Concepts) [ITIL Concepts]

Knowledge Area Quiz: Service Management Practices

Test Name: Knowledge Area Quiz: Service Management Practices
Total Questions: 10
Correct Answers Needed to Pass: 7 (70.00%)
Time Allowed: 10 Minutes

Test Description

This practice test targets the Service Management Practices of ITIL.

Test Questions

1. The IT Asset Manager is responsible for:

   A. Consolidating servers to save money.

   B. Recording the relationships between service assets and configuration items

   C. Full lifecycle management of IT and Service assets from acquisitions to disposal

   D. Configuration auditing

2. American Title Company is experiencing an outage on its internet circuit. Their service provider has indicated that it will not be resolved within the range of the American Title Company's SLA, and as a result the situation is escalated to management for resolution. What is this type of escalation called?

   A. Executive Escalation

   B. Priority Escalation

   C. Hierarchical Escalation

   D. Functional Escalation

3. Monitoring and optimizing the performance of infrastructure components required to support IT services is the responsibility of which ITIL role?

   A. Incident Manager

   B. Capacity and Performance Manager

   C. Service Desk Manager

   D. IT Operations Manager

4. Monitoring and Event Management can be applied to which of the following aspects of Service Management? I) Configuration items II) Environmental conditions III) Software license monitoring IV) Security

   A. I, II and IV

   B. All of them

   C. II, III and IV

   D. I, II and III

5. A service outage has occurred at Red River Systems. The outage had minimal impact on mission critical services, but it did hinder the ability of many users to access files needed for week-ending processes. The root cause was discovered, and a plan was put in place to correct the underlying problem and ensure that it does not happen again. What is this plan called?

   A. Configuration Management Plan

   B. Business Service Continuity Plan

   C. Service Level Plan

   D. Service Improvement Plan

6. The Service Continuity Management Practice is implemented and managed in which of these Categories of ITIL Practices?

   A. Service Management Practices

   B. Technical Management Practices

   C. General Management Practices

   D. Service Design

7. WebSphere Hosting, a web site hosting company, received a support request from one of its clients. The client requested that a backup of their web site's database be made available for download. A look at the SLA shows that this request should be accommodated by WebSphere Hosting within 24 hours. How best can this request be categorized?

   A. A Known Error

   B. A Service Level Requirement

   C. A Change Request

   D. A Service Request

8. _____ can be described as a result of Lloyd's car wash output.

Knowledge Area Quiz: Service Management Practices - Practice Questions

A. Relationship

B. Outcome

C. Service Provision

D. A Product

D. Service Operation

9. In ITIL 4, by adopting the _____, an organization ensures a holistic approach to Service Management

   A. Four Perspectives

   B. Deming Cycle

   C. Five Aspects of Service Design

   D. Four Dimensions of Service Management

10. Service Portfolio Management, identification of business requirements, technology architectural design, process design, and measurement design are five critical aspects of what practice in service management?

    A. Service Strategy

    B. Service Transition

    C. Service Design

Knowledge Area Quiz: Service Management Practices Answer Key and Explanations

1. C - IT Asset Management is responsible for the management of service assets across the whole lifecycle and maintenance of the asset inventory. (Service Management Practices) [Service Management Practices]

2. C - Hierarchical or Vertical Escalations are used to escalate an issue to authorized line management when resolution of an Incident will not be in time or satisfactory according to the terms of the SLA. (Service Management Practices) [Service Management Practices]

3. B - The Capacity and Performance Manager is responsible for ensuring adequate and appropriate performance and capacity for all IT services. (Service Management Practices) [Service Management Practices]

4. B - Monitoring and Event Management can be applied to all the following aspects of Service management. I) Configuration items II) Environmental conditions. III) Software license monitoring. IV). Security. (Service Management Practices) [Service Management Practices]

5. D - Service Improvement Plans are formal plans to implement improvements to a process or service. They are used to ensure that improvement actions are identified and carried out on a regular basis. (Service Management Practices) [Service Management Practices]

6. A - Service Continuity Management is implemented and managed in the Service Management Practices Category. (Service Management Practices) [Service Management Practices]

7. D - ITIL defines standard services which are agreed to in the SLA as Service Requests. Service Requests are handled using the Incident Management Practice tracking tool. (Service Management Practices) [Service Management Practices]

8. B - One output of Lloyd's car wash is a clean car and can be referred to as the output of their services. (Service Management Practices) [Service Management Practices]

9. D - The Four Dimensions of Service Management ensures a holistic approach to Service Management.

(Service Management Practices) [Service Management Practices]

10. C - These activities are critical to Service Design. On its own, Service Portfolio Management is a key process associated with service strategy. When applied in conjunction with the four additional activities stated, it becomes a critical aspect of Service Design. (Service Management Practices) [Service Management Practices]

ITIL Foundation Mock Exam (LITE) - 5

Test Name: ITIL Foundation Mock Exam (LITE) - 5
Total Questions: 40
Correct Answers Needed to Pass: 30 (75.00%)
Time Allowed: 60 Minutes

Test Description

This is the fifth cumulative ITIL Foundation test which can be used as an indicator for overall performance. This practice test includes questions from key ITIL areas.

Test Questions

1. John is part of an engineering and architecture team designing the network infrastructure for a new service offering. In what ITIL Practice is this work being conducted?

   A. IT Asset Management

   B. Availability Management

   C. Strategy Management

   D. Architecture Management

2. What type of analysis must be conducted before implementing a security measure?

   A. Cost- Benefit Analysis

   B. SWOT

   C. ROI

   D. RACI

3. What role is responsible for documenting and publicizing processes, defining and reviewing KPIs for a given process, and contributing input to an ongoing Service Improvement Plan.

   A. Service Owner

   B. Service Level Manager

   C. Process Owner

   D. Change Manager

4. Which of the following CORRECTLY describe the Four Dimensions of ITSM?

   A. Partners-People-Profession-Process

B. Profession-Planning-Process-Pride

C. Organizations & People; Information & Technology; Partners & Suppliers; Value Streams & Processes

D. Partners-Planning-Products-Process

5. Under ITIL, how is the value of a service defined?

   A. Through business outcomes and customer perception

   B. Through revenue and profit generated

   C. Through consistency and quality

   D. Through service cost and demand

6. Capital, infrastructure, applications, and information are examples of _____.

   A. Resources

   B. Supplies

   C. Capabilities

   D. Capacity

7. Adding additional support capacity, such as extended Service Desk hours, often increases the demand for additional support mechanisms such as a self-service webpage. The increased use of these support services justifies the costs associated with maintenance and upgrades, further enhancing the potential for better performance. This is an example of:

   A. An adaptive system

   B. A closed-loop control system

   C. Management by design

   D. Good planning

8. Dynamic Data implemented a change in its network, but discovered that the change caused unplanned service interruptions. Because the extent of the interruptions is unknown, the implementation team decides to abort the change and recover to the last known good configuration noted in the change plan. What is this process called?

   A. Service Incident

   B. Modeling

C. Remediation

D. Outcome Facilitation

9. Senior management has been analyzing the types of calls logged by the Service Desk at West Coast Manufacturing. A significant percentage of the calls were found to be related to forgotten passwords and requests for new software on users' workstations. It is determined that a webpage to let users reset their passwords and request new software will be a useful service to deploy company wide. What is this type of support called?

   A. Single Sign-on

   B. Intranet

   C. Self-Help

   D. Service Desk

10. A monitoring system at HostIT INC indicated that a recent change to the infrastructure resulted in the failure of five client servers. To plan the next course of action, HostIT needs to act immediately, and does not have time to coordinate a formal review of next steps. Under ITIL, what is the name of the group of people HostIT will assemble to review these highly urgent changes?

    A. Change Authority

    B. CAB-EC

    C. CAB

    D. ACB

11. Setting an annual budget for the cost of improving existing services is an often overlooked planning process. By having funding in place, the Continual Improvement team can take _____ action to trends discovered through analysis of performance metrics.

    A. Strategic

    B. Proactive

    C. Reactive

    D. Decisive

12. Markham Management has contracted with Diamond Data Systems to provide 24x7x365, 4-hour response, on-site service for Markham's networking equipment. This contract is renewed annually, and Markham may add equipment to the contract at

any time. What role does Diamond Data Systems play in this scenario?

A. Warranty Provider

B. Service Provider

C. Underpinning Contractor

D. Supplier

13. Moving changes into the live environment can be referred to as _____.

A. Change

B. Backout

C. Release

D. Deployment

14. George's business services use a combination of people, teams, and value streams with a blended approach to service management. This approach takes advantage of the _____ _____ of service management

A. Six Steps

B. Five Aspects

C. Five Dimensions

D. Four Dimensions

15. Informatic Systems has deployed a database that tracks all Incidents and Problems that have occurred, as well as information such as root cause and resolution. This system helps staff reach a faster diagnosis and resolution for future of Incidents and Problems. What is this database called?

A. Known Error Database

B. Knowledgebase

C. Configuration Management Database

D. Incident Log

16. Which Service Management Practice ensures that information in the Service Catalog regarding services which run in the live environment is current and accurate?

A. Service Validation and Testing

B. Availability Management

C. Service Catalogue Management

D. Service Level Management

17. Service or Business value is always in the perception of the customer. This statement translates to and leads us to which of the following statements?

    A. If the services generate more value to the customer, this strengthens the business relations and the bond between the business and the customer.

    B. If the services are available at very cheap cost, the customer will be hesitant to place repeat orders and recommend other clients.

    C. If you give (good or bad) service to the customer, he will give you more business.

    D. You must always please the clients to get more business.

18. What practice is used by an organization to meet the objectives of confidentiality, information integrity, information availability, and authenticity of information?

    A. Service Level Management

    B. Availability Management

    C. Information Security Management

    D. Supplier Management

19. Gary is the Continual Improvement Manager for High Point Electronics. He implemented a customer service improvement plan three months ago, which set a target of 20% increase in customer satisfaction. He implemented a new customer satisfaction survey to determine the answer to Step 6 of the Continual Improvement Plan, which asks ___ ___ ___ ____?

    A. How do we get there?

    B. Did we get there?

    C. Where do we want to be?

    D. Where are we now?

20. Connecting Point has decided to bundle a set number of additional support hours beyond the basic support included with their Managed Hosting offering to stand out from their competitors' service offerings. This is called:

    A. Delivery of Value through core services

    B. Service Design.

C. The Formative Theorem

D. Developing a differentiated offering

21. The Continual Improvement Model summarizes the ongoing improvement cycle. This approach starts with what important question?

    A. Where are we going?

    B. What is the vision?

    C. Are we under or over budget?

    D. What services are we offering?

22. Posting a patch or updated driver on a website where users can download and install the software at their discretion is known as what type of release?

    A. Manual Approach

    B. Pull Approach

    C. Push Approach

    D. Phased Approach

23. Availability performance is measured and reported in several ways. Two measurements are ____ and ____.

    A. MTBF and MTRS

    B. Continual Improvement

    C. Capacity and Performance

    D. Portfolio Management

24. Which of the following is the correct order of activities in the Service Request Practice? I) Initiation, II) Approval, III) Fulfilment, IV) Management?

    A. I-II-III-IV

    B. II-I-III-IV

    C. III-II-I-IV

    D. I-II-IV-III

25. The two types of assets are _____ and _____.

    A. Goods and services

    B. Quantifiable and qualitative

    C. Resources and capabilities

D. Skills and manufacturing capacity

26. A pilot launch occurs during which practice?

    A. Service Operation

    B. Continual Service Improvement

    C. Release Management

    D. Service Design

27. Prioritization of an incident is based on which two factors?

    A. Outage Duration and Number of Users Affected

    B. SLA and Guarantees

    C. Value and Warranty

    D. Impact and Urgency

28. Which item does not reflect a component of Warranty, or fitness for use?

    A. Availability

    B. Utility

    C. Continuity

    D. Capacity

29. A service provider wants to identify the roles of the stakeholders of a new product it will offer. Which of the following models would be useful for this purpose?

    A. FMIT

    B. Flowchart

    C. RACI

    D. Swim-lane

30. Leggett Accounting has found that its corporate email system has consistently fallen below stated levels of availability. Which of the following would be developed to determine how best to improve email services?

    A. Service Improvement Plan

    B. Capacity Management Plan

    C. Service Metric Analysis

    D. Availability Management Plan

31. A managed hosting provider needs a more robust network monitoring tool. Which process would be used to gather data to help the organization determine if it is more appropriate to buy a commercial tool or develop one in house?

A. Portfolio Management

B. Service Financial Management

C. Budgeting

D. Demand Management

32. Plan, Do, Check, Act are the four phases of which continuous process improvement model?

A. Maslow's Hierarchy

B. ITIL

C. Ishikawa Model

D. Deming Cycle

33. Which of the following is not a key metric associated with Service Level Management?

A. SLA Breaches in Underpinning Contracts

B. SLA Targets Missed

C. Incidents due to Capacity Shortages

D. Customer Satisfaction of SLA Achievements

34. Which of the following statements does NOT form an input to the Continual Improvement Process?

A. The need to do business

B. The drive to reduce cost

C. The desire to improve operational efficiency

D. The need to improve

35. The DIKW structure is used for _____.

A. Protection of intellectual property

B. Training and knowledge transfer

C. Visualizing knowledge management

D. Documentation of errors, workarounds, and test information

ITIL Foundation Mock Exam (LITE) 5 - Practice Questions

36. The law firm of Tregoe and Lawton has a large number of case records to be entered into their document management system on a daily basis. The amount of bandwidth used to send imaged documents to the documentation repository slows down all other functions during peak use times. The IT department determines the most cost effective way to eliminate this problem is to batch the images for transfer after hours. What is this called?

A. Task Switching

B. Job Scheduling

C. Job Sharing

D. Batch Processing

37. What types of incidents should be logged by the Service Desk?

A. Only incidents which require functional escalation

B. All incidents should be logged by the Service Desk

C. Only incidents which cannot be resolved by the Service Desk personnel

D. All incidents excluding Service Requests

38. Which of the following indicates that the service is fit for the purpose for which it was designed?

A. Warranty

B. Available

C. Utility

D. Value

39. Which of the following ITIL Practices is most heavily aligned with the Plan, Do, Check, Act (PDCA) model?

A. Continual Improvement

B. Strategy Management

C. Change Control

D. Service Design

40. Which of the following statements is a CORRECT definition of an Event in ITIL 4?

A. An Event is a change of state that has significance for the management of a service in

Service Catalog Management process.

B. An Event is a change of process state that has significance for IT Management within an organization.

C. An Event is a change of state that has significance for the Configuration Management Practice.

D. An Event is a change of state that has significance for the management of a configuration item or IT service.

ITIL Foundation Mock Exam (LITE) - 5 Answer Key and Explanations

1. B - The infrastructure, processes, and support mechanisms needed to meet the availability requirements of the customer are developed during the Availability Management Practice. (Service Management Practices) [Service Management Practices]

2. A - A cost-benefit analysis must be conducted before implementing a security measure, to ensure the measure is appropriate for both the threat risk and potential loss. (General Management Practices) [General Management Practices]

3. C - The Process Owner is responsible for the activities listed above. In addition, the Process Owner must address process issues, and ensure sufficient staff exists to carry out specific processes. (Service Management Practices) [Service Management Practices]

4. C - Organizations & People; Information & Technology; Partners & Suppliers; Value Streams & Processes correctly describe the Four Dimensions of ITSM. (ITIL Concepts) [ITIL Concepts]

5. A - Value is defined by the business outcomes achieved and the customer's perception of that outcome. (ITIL Concepts) [ITIL Concepts]

6. A - Resources are the direct inputs for production, and, together with capabilities, form the basis for the value of a service. (ITIL Concepts) [ITIL Concepts]

7. B - Service Management is a closed-loop control system with the following functions: developing and understanding service assets; understanding the performance potential of customer assets; mapping of Service Assets to Customer Assets through services, and designing, developing, and adapting services. (Service Management Practices) [Service Management Practices]

8. C - Remediation is recovery to a known state after a failed Change or Release. (ITIL Concept) [ITIL Concepts]

9. C - Many organizations find it beneficial to offer Self Help capabilities such as web pages to their users. This reduces the load on the Service Desk and can lead to greater efficiency in user requests being fulfilled. (Service Management Practices) [Service Management Practices]

10. A - A Change Authority will be assembled immediately, as the change is critical and cannot wait for a formal Change Authority meeting. (Service Management Practices) [Service Management Practices]

11. B - It is recommended that an annual budget is set for the Service Improvement Plan (SIP) to permit quick actions to mitigate potential service Incidents, rather than reacting to service outages that have already occurred. (Service Management Practices) [Service Management Practices]

12. D - Suppliers are third-party organizations that provide essential goods or services to support another organization's service offering. In this case, Diamond Data Systems supplies services for the infrastructure resources that make up Markham's network. (General Management Practices) [General Management Practices]

13. D - Deployment Management is the Practice of actually moving the Change from the Development state to the live infrastructure and available for consumption. (Service Management Practices) [Service Management Practices]

14. D - The Four Dimensions of Service Management uses a blended approach to provide George's business services. (ITIL Concepts) [ITIL Concepts]

15. A - The purpose of a Known Error Database is to store knowledge about Incidents and Problems and how they were remedied, so that a quicker diagnosis and solution can be found if further Incidents and Problems occur. (Service Management Practices) [Service Management Practices]

16. C - Service Catalogue Management ensures that information regarding services which run in the live environment is current and accurate. (Service Management Practices) [Service Management Practices]

17. A - If the services generate more value to the customer, this strengthens the business relations and the bond between the business and the customer. (Service Management Practices) [Service Management Practices]

18. C - Information Security Management supports the main objectives of confidentiality, integrity, availability, and authenticity. (Service Management Practices) [Service Management Practices]

19. B - Step 6 of the Continual Improvement Plan asks the question, "Did we get there?" (General Management Practices) [General Management Practices]

20. D - Bundling Core services and Supporting Services are a vital aspect of a market strategy. Service providers should thoroughly analyze the primary conditions in their business environment, the needs of the customer segments or types they serve, and the alternatives available to these customers. (ITIL Concepts) [ITIL Concepts]

21. B - The Continual Improvement Model uses a series of questions to gather and analyze information about existing IT services and subsequently make plans to develop and improve services. Touching all areas of ITIL practices, these questions are: What is the vision? Where are we now? Where do we want to be? How do we get there? Take Action. Did we get there? How Do We Keep the Momentum Going? (ITIL Concepts) [ITIL Concepts]

22. B - The Pull Approach is characterized by the posting of a software release in a central location for users to download and install on their own timetable. (Generic Concepts and Definitions) [Generic Concepts and Definitions]

23. A - Service Availability can be measured in many ways. Some measurements are Meantime Between Failures (MTBF) or uptime, Meantime to Restore Service (MTRS), Meantime to Repair (MTTR), and Meantime to Diagnose MTTD). (Service Management Practices) [Service Management Practices]

24. A - The following is the CORRECT order of activities in the Service Request Practice: I) Initiation, II) Approval, III) Fulfilment, IV) Management. (Service Management Practices) [Service Management Practices]

25. C - Resources and capabilities are types of assets. Organizations use them to create value in the form of goods and services. (ITIL Concepts) [ITIL Concepts]

26. C - Release Management activities include the management and coordination of the processes, systems, and functions required for the building and testing, of a release into production. (Service Management Practices) [Service Management Practices]

27. D - Prioritization is based on the impact (degree to which the user is affected) and urgency (degree to which resolution can be delayed). (ITIL Concepts) [ITIL Concepts]

28. B - The primary concepts which represent Warranty are Availability, Capacity, Continuity, and Security. (ITIL Concepts) [ITIL Concepts]

29. C - A RACI model is used to document roles and relationships between stakeholders. Stakeholders are identified as one or more of the following: Responsible, Accountable, Consulted, and Informed. Only one person can hold the role of "Accountable". (Generic Concepts and Definitions) [Generic Concepts and Definitions]

30. A - Service Improvement Plans are used to implement necessary changes to improve a service. A baseline measurement is used as a reference point to determine if improvement goals have been met. (ITIL Concepts) [ITIL Concepts]

31. B - The Service Financial Management Practice is used to estimate the cost to deliver a service, the data that is subsequently used to develop business models, and cost benefit analyses. (General Management Practices) [General Management Practices]

32. D - The Deming Cycle, also known as PDCA, is a continuous process improvement model. Each step is carried out in this specific order, as many times as necessary. (Generic Concepts and Definitions) [Generic Concepts and Definitions]

33. C - The number of Incidents due to Capacity shortages would not be tracked by Service Level Management; rather it would be tracked by Capacity and Performance Management. (Service Management Practices) [Service Management Practices]

34. A - The need to do business is NOT an input to the ITIL Continual Improvement Practice. (General Management Practices) [General Management Practices]

35. C - Knowledge management is often visualized using the DIKW structure: Data-Information-Knowledge-Wisdom. (Generic Concepts and Definitions) [Generic Concepts and Definitions]

36. B - Job scheduling is the planning and management of software tasks that are required as part of an IT Service. Job Scheduling is carried out by IT operations management and is often automated using software tools that run batch or online tasks at specific

times of the day, week, month, or year. (Service Management Practices) [Service Management Practices]

37. B - As the correct response indicates, all incidents should be logged by the Service Desk. (Service Management Practices) [Service Management Practices]

38. C - Utility defines the functionality of an IT service from the customer's perspective, ensuring that the desired performance is supported, and constraints have been removed. (ITIL Concepts) [ITIL Concepts]

39. A - Continual Service Improvement is heavily aligned with the Plan, Do, Check, Act (PDCA) model. (General Management Practices) [General Management Practices]

40. D - The CORRECT definition of an Event in ITIL 4 is: "An event is a change of state that has significance for the management of a configuration item or IT service." (Service Management Practices) [Service Management Practices]

Knowledge Area Quiz: Service Value Chain (SVC)

Test Name: Knowledge Area Quiz: Service Value Chain (SVC)
Total Questions: 12
Correct Answers Needed to Pass: 8 (66.67%)
Time Allowed: 15 Minutes

Test Description

This practice test focuses specifically on ITIL's Service Value Chain (SVC).

Test Questions

1. The Service Value Chain activity that deals with customer negotiation is the _____ activity.

    A. Engage

    B. Supplier Management

    C. Service Level Management

    D. Deliver & Support

2. The Service Value Chain activity that provides an operating model for the creation, delivery and continual improvement of customer services is included in the _____ activity.

    A. Technological Factors

    B. Customer Service

    C. Products & Services

    D. Dimensions

3. Which activity of the Value Chain activities includes negotiating Supplier Contracts?

    A. Obtain & Build

    B. Deliver & Support

    C. Engage

    D. Output

4. Getting data from the source helps avoid assumptions that, if unfounded, can be disastrous to the quality of the results.

    A. CMS

    B. Start Where You Are

    C. Optimize and Automate

    D. CMDB

Knowledge Area Quiz: SVC - Service Value Chain - Practice Questions

5. The Service Value Chain activities include: Improve, Engage, Design & Transition, Obtain/Build, Deliver & Support and _____.

   A. Governance

   B. Availability

   C. Plan

   D. Practices

6. To ensure service components meet their purpose and are available is an activity of what value chain activity.

   A. Availability Management

   B. Design and Transition

   C. Deliver and Support

   D. Obtain/build

7. Which Value Chain Activity uses service components to fulfill Service Requests?

   A. Obtain/build

   B. Deliver & Support

   C. Design & Transition

   D. Engage

8. When designing service management agreements, which of the following dimensions must be considered? I) Organizations & People, II) Information & Technology, III) Partners & Suppliers, IV) Value Streams & Processes

   A. All of them

   B. II, III

   C. I only

   D. IV only

9. The purpose of the _____ activity of the Service Value Chain is to provide an understanding of the overall vision, direction and current status.

   A. Improve

   B. Plan

   C. Engage

   D. Deliver & Support

Knowledge Area Quiz: SVC - Service Value Chain - Practice Questions

10. Which value chain activity ensures people understand the organization's vision?

A. Obtain/Build

B. Deliver and Support

C. Plan

D. Improve

Knowledge Area Quiz:
SVC - Service Value Chain
Answer Key and Explanations

1. A - The Service Value Chain activity that deals with customer negotiation is the Engage activity. (SVC) [SVC - Service Value Chain]

2. C - Products & Services are produced through the activities of the Service Value Chain. (SVC) [SVC - Service Value Chain]

3. C - Negotiating Supplier Contracts is performed as part of the "Engage" Value Chain Activity. (SVC) [SVC - Service Value Chain]

4. B - The "Start Where You Are" Guiding Principle recommends that services already in place should be measured and/or observed directly to understand their current state and what can be reused. (SVC) [SVC - Service Value Chain]

5. C - The Service Value Chain activities include: Plan, Improve, Engage, Design & Transition, Obtain/Build, and Deliver & Support. (SVC) [SVC - Service Value Chain]

6. D - The Obtain/build activity of the Value Chain ensures the service components meet the purpose and availability requirements of the service. (SVC) [SVC - Service Value Chain]

7. A - The Obtain/build activity of the Value Chain ensures the service components meet the purpose and availability requirements of the service. (SVC) [SVC - Service Value Chain]

8. A - When designing service management agreements, we must consider the holistic view of the Four Dimensions of Service Management. (SVC) [SVC - Service Value Chain]

9. B - The Service Chain Activity "Plan" begins with an understanding of the current status of the overall stakeholder vision and direction. (SVC) [SVC - Service Value Chain]

10. C - The purpose of the Plan value chain activity is "to ensure a shared understanding of the vision, current status, and improvement direction." (SVC) [SVC - Service Value Chain]

Learning Outcomes

1. Key Service Management Concepts (Ch. 2)
2. ITIL guiding principals (Ch. 4)
3. 4 Dimensions of Service Management (Ch. 3)
4. ITIL Service Value System (Ch. 4.1)
5. Service Value Change (Ch 4.5)
6. 15 ITIL practices (Ch 5)
7. 7 ITIL practices (Ch 4/5)

Exam prep
   Foundation - pg. 6 - Baseline (after reading)

Chapter

ITIL Foundation Mock Exam (LITE) - 6

Test Name: ITIL Foundation Mock Exam (LITE) - 6
Total Questions: 40
Correct Answers Needed to Pass: 30 (75.00%)
Time Allowed: 60 Minutes

Test Description

This is the sixth cumulative ITIL Foundation test which can be used as an indicator for overall performance. This practice test includes questions from key ITIL areas.

Test Questions

1. Which is the correct definition of a Configuration Item in ITIL?

   A. A Configuration Item (CI) is a policy or rule which must be under the control of Service Configuration Management.

   B. A Configuration Item (CI) is an asset, service component or other item which is, or will be, under the control of Service Configuration Management.

   C. A Configuration Item (CI) is an integral part of Service Configuration Management process which will help identify errors in the system.

   D. A Configuration Item (CI) is a document or a file which is, or will be, under the control of Service Configuration Management.

2. What are the four main roles of the RACI model?

   A. Responsible, Accountable, Consulted, Informed

   B. Plan, Do, Check, Act

   C. Review, Audit, Confirm, Implement

   D. Revenue, Accounting, Control, Investments

3. Fitness for use, or the assurance that products and services provided will meet certain specifications, reflects which concept below?

   A. Warranty

   B. Utility

   C. Resources

D. Service Management

4. Controlling demand for a service can be done with which two ways?

    A. Calculation-based Constraints, Impact-based Constraints

    B. Technical Constraints, Financial Constraints

    C. Internal Constraints, External Constraints

    D. Strategic Constraints, Tactical Constraints

5. What practice is responsible for managing the lifecycle of all Service Requests.

    A. Service/Portfolio Management

    B. Service Desk

    C. Incident Management

    D. Service Request Management

6. The phrase, "A fool with a tool is still a ____", means that it takes more than technology to make a difference.

    A. Fool

    B. Tool

    C. Ghoul

    D. Jewel

7. A planned recovery from a disaster in >72 hours is called what?

    A. Gradual

    B. Reciprocal

    C. Manual

    D. Intermediate

8. Service Continuity Management would not focus on:

    A. Email system failure

    B. An unplanned shutoff of water service to the call center due to storm damage in the area.

    C. Installation of cubicles in a disaster recovery data center.

    D. Merging the IT departments of two different organizations as part of a corporate acquisition.

9. Ralph is embarking on an improvement project and after studying the Continual Improvement Model, has determined that the starting point would be to begin with a current state assessment which would answer the question: _____ __ __ ___?

    A. Where do we want to be?

    B. What is the plan?

    C. Are we there yet?

    D. Where are we now?

10. Each department at Regional Construction is charged $0.01 per page printed. These charges are deducted from each department's shared services budget. What practice is responsible for developing and implementing this charging system?

    A. Business service management

    B. Cost center management

    C. Accounting controls

    D. Service Financial Management

11. Connaught Construction conducts a quarterly management meeting to review how well current IT services are meeting the current needs of the business, as well as identifying potential new needs. This activity falls within the scope of which ITIL Practice?

    A. Availability Management

    B. IT Asset Management

    C. General Management

    D. Continual Improvement

12. ITIL describes a model for ensuring a service is ready for release to customers that involves specifying and validating all requirements. What is this model called?

    A. Matrix

    B. Iterative

    C. Waterfall

    D. Service V Model

13. The Service Catalog contains an organization's Business Services Catalog and Technical Service Catalog, both of which contain details of all the

IT services delivered to the customer, each from a different perspective. The Business Service Catalog provides what view of the Service Catalog?

A. Departmental view

B. Customer view

C. Contract view

D. Shared Services view

14. Richard maintains a large inventory of spare parts for the systems in his company's IT infrastructure. These spares include disk drives, network switches, and VoIP phones, all of which are pre-configured and ready to be put into production. Where is the information regarding this inventory documented?

A. Hardware Library

B. Configuration Management System

C. Just In Time Inventory

D. Hot Spares

15. Delta Solutions is in the process of developing a new Internet phone service which will allow customers to make telephone calls directly from their web browser. This new service will be available to customers in the European market only. Delta Solutions plans to release the service within the next six to twelve months. Where is this service most likely tracked by Delta Solutions?

A. Service Lifecycle

B. Service Pipeline

C. Retired Services

D. Service Catalogue

16. What term best represents a component of the Service Knowledge Management System where supplier contracts are managed throughout their lifecycle?

A. Supplier and Contract Database

B. Service Catalogue

C. Service Portfolio

D. Supplier Catalogue

17. Change Control Practices are executed by the _____ _____ role, which is defined by the type and circumstances of the Change.

A. Change Manager

B. Change Initiator

C. Change Advisor

D. Change Authority

18. Lifeline Industries has developed a matrix to define the roles and responsibilities of individual staff or entire groups in relationship to processes and activities. What is the matrix called?

A. Service Matrix

B. Organization Chart

C. Rummler-Brache Diagram

D. RACI Model

19. After conducting a Business Impact Analysis on the Balfour Glassware Corporation's IT infrastructure, it is determined that in the event of a disaster, certain file servers can be brought back up online several days after the rest of the organizations' more critical assets. What is this type of recovery called?

A. Manual Recovery

B. Interim Recovery

C. Gradual Recovery

D. Intermediate Recovery

20. Western Enterprises is evaluating new technology for implementation in their service environment. Which of the following practices is concerned with this evaluation?

A. Service Capacity Management

B. Capacity and Performance Management

C. Engineering Capacity Management

D. Technical Capacity Management

21. Service Performance is highly dependent upon the _____ of resources available.

A. Value

B. Capacity

C. Status

D. Sourcing

ITIL Foundation Mock Exam (LITE) 6 - Practice Questions

22. Customer needs are identified in which practice?

   A. Customer service management
   B. Service Design
   C. Service Strategy
   D. Relationship management

23. What term indicates "fitness for use"?

   A. Liability
   B. Warranty
   C. Guarantee
   D. Utility

24. Worldwide Mergers and Acquisitions is rolling out a new service offering. In which phase will analysis of the service offering be most useful?

   A. Planning phase
   B. Measurement phase
   C. Implementation phase
   D. All of the above

25. Which of the following items below would least likely be categorized as a Service Request?

   A. A request to fix a user's network connection which failed after an application caused an error
   B. A request for a password re-set to allow a user to log in to a time tracking program
   C. A request for a user manual for the corporate extranet
   D. A request for a database extract from an information system

26. With which of the following groups must the Change Control Team most closely coordinate?

   A. Executives
   B. IT Staff
   C. Customers
   D. None of the above

27. Taking in to account the use of baseline data under Continual Improvement, which of the statements below are true?   a. If the integrity of measurement data is questionable, it is better to not have any data at all. b. If a baseline has not yet been established, the first measurements will immediately become the baseline

A. A and B

B. A

C. B

D. None of the above are true.

28. What role is responsible for managing and maintaining the business and technical Service Catalogue while ensuring all information is consistent with that of the Service Portfolio?

A. Demand Manager

B. Service Catalogue Manager

C. Service Level Manager

D. Product Manager

29. Acme Enterprises IT group has an SLA with all its internal customers guaranteeing that services will be available Monday-Friday, 8am-5pm. A team within the IT group constantly monitors all aspects of the service offering to be sure that the appropriate resources and infrastructure are in place to meet or exceed the terms of the SLA. What is the name of this process?

A. Service Reviews

B. Service Analysis

C. Availability Management

D. Capacity Management

30. Which of the statements below are true regarding service assets? a. The justification to maintain and upgrade service assets is increased as the demand for those service assets increase b. Costs incurred by accommodating the demand for services can be recovered from the customer through agreed terms and conditions

A. Both statements are false

B. A

C. B

D. A and B

31. HostIT INC has defined a set of activities for its System Administrators

to follow when provisioning server space for a new account. As such, HostIT is able to consistently describe what has to be done, what the expected results are, and how to measure the performance of the newly provisioned account. What is the ITIL term used to represent a structured set of activities designed to accomplish a defined objective?

A. Process

B. Work Instruction

C. Value

D. Procedure

32. Which of the following types of support models offers the highest First Call Resolution rate?

A. Customer Service Group

B. Help Desk

C. Call Center

D. Service Desk

33. According to the Deming quality circle, a number of steps must be performed repeatedly in order to ensure good performance. Which of the following are the correct sequence of steps?

A. Act-Check-Do-Plan

B. Do-Plan-Check-Act

C. Check-Plan-Act-Do

D. Plan- Do-Check-Act

34. Which of the statements below describe the value offered to customers through the use of an IT Service? a. Performance of associated tasks are enhanced b. The probability of desired outcomes on behalf of the customer is increased   c. Customer risk is increased, along with a higher potential for reward   d. The effect of constraints is reduced

A. A, C, D

B. B, C, D

C. A, B, D

D. All of these responses / All of the above

35. Information Security must maintain a balance between: I) Prevention II)Technical III) Detection IV) Correction

A. I, III, IV

B. I, IV

C. II, IV

D. III, IV

36. In ITIL, what is the generic sequence of events which take place in a Process Model? a. Data enters b. Data is processed c. Data is measured and reviewed d. Data is output

A. A, B, C, D

B. A, D, B, C

C. A, C, B, D

D. A, B, D, C

37. What ITIL Practice acts as a single point of contact for IT users on a day to day basis?

A. IT Operations Management

B. Service Desk

C. Incident Management

D. Application Management

38. Which role is responsible for ensuring that the Service Catalog is in sync with the Portfolio?

A. The Service Design Manager

B. The Service Level Manager

C. The Service Catalog Manager

D. The Availability Manager

39. Which of the statements below concerning Value Creation are true? a. An organization uses Service Assets to create value in the form of goods and services. b. An organization relies on Capabilities to coordinate, control, and deploy Resources to produce value.

A. A and B

B. A

C. B

D. None of the above are true.

40. What is the name of the formal plan to implement improvements to an IT Service, and is an output of the Continual Improvement Plan?

ITIL Foundation Mock Exam (LITE) 6 - Practice Questions

A. RACI

B. Service Improvement Plan (SIP)

C. Release Plan

D. Request for Change (RFC)

ITIL Foundation Mock Exam (LITE) - 6 Answer Key and Explanations

1. B - The correct definition of a Configuration Item in ITIL V4 is : "A Configuration Item (CI) is an asset, service component or other item which is, or will be, under the control of Service Configuration Management." (Service Management Practices) [Service Management Practices]

2. A - The four main roles of the RACI model are Responsible, Accountable, Consulted, Informed. (Generic Concepts and Definitions) [Generic Concepts and Definitions]

3. A - Warranty reflects "fitness for use" and assures customers that certain specifications are met for products or services; also, performance variation is reduced with warranty. (ITIL Concepts) [ITIL Concepts]

4. B - Demand for a service can be influenced or managed through technical constraints such as bandwidth throttling or financial constraints such as charging higher service rates for usage during peak hours. (Service Management Practices) [Service Management Practices]

5. D - Service Request Management is responsible for managing the overall lifecycle of all Service Requests. (ITIL Concepts) [ITIL Concepts]

6. A - The phrase, "A fool with a tool is still a fool", means that it takes more than technology to make a difference. (Generic Concepts and Definitions) [Generic Concepts and Definitions]

7. A - A Gradual Recovery, also known as a Cold Recovery, offers >72 hour recovery from a disaster. (Service Management Practices) [Service Management Practices]

8. D - Service Continuity Management focuses on those events that can be considered a disaster, not small technical problems that are handled by Incident Management. (Service Management Practices) [Service Management Practices]

9. D - The Continual Improvement Model begins with assessing the current state by answering the question "Where are we now?" (General Management Practices) [General Management Practices]

10. D - Service Financial Management ensures that the appropriate level of funding to design ,develop, and deliver IT services is secured. Funding models can include charging,

which is requiring customers to pay for the services that they use. (General Management Practices) [General Management Practices]

11. D - Ongoing alignment of services with current and future business needs is one of the objectives of the Continual Improvement practice. (Service Management Practices) [Service Management Practices]

12. D - The Service V Model is a structured approach to defining acceptance requirements against requirements for features, functionality, performance. When the acceptance requirements for all aspects of the service have been met, the service is deemed ready for release to customers. (ITIL Concepts) [ITIL Concepts]

13. B - The Business Service Catalog contains the relationships between business units and business processes that rely on IT services, and is the customer view of the Service Catalog. (Service Management Practices) [Service Management Practices]

14. B - Information regarding spare equipment and components that are preconfigured and maintained at the same level as the production environment are housed in a secure location with information documented in the CMS. (ITIL Concepts) [ITIL Concepts]

15. B - The Service Pipeline reflects services that are still in development for a specific customer or market. (ITIL Concepts) [ITIL Concepts]

16. A - The Supplier Contract Database is used to manage the entire lifecycle of supplier contracts, and is a component of the Service Knowledge Management System. (General Management Practices) [General Management Practices]

17. D - The Change Authority is determined by the type and circumstances of the proposed change. (Service Management Practices) [Service Management Practices]

18. D - The RACI Model (AKA Authority Matrix) is used to define roles and responsibilities of people or groups in relation to processes and activities. It defines who is responsible, accountable, consulted, and informed for a specific action or event. (Generic Concepts and Definitions) [Generic Concepts and Definitions]

19. C - A gradual recovery from a disaster offers recovery times in terms of days, rather than hours. Systems and services are returned to service in >72

hours. (Service Management Practices) [Service Management Practices]

20. B - Capacity and Performance Management identifies and manages each of the components of the IT Infrastructure such as CPU, memory, bandwidth and evaluates new technologies. (Service Management Practices) [Service Management Practices]

21. B - Service Performance is highly dependent upon the Capacity of resources available. (Service Management Practices) [Service Management Practices]

22. D - Relationship management is the practice by which customer needs are identified. This process is also responsible for ensuring that these needs are met. (General Management Practices) [General Management Practices]

23. B - ITIL uses two important concepts for the value of a service. For customers, the positive effect is the "utility" of a service; the insurance of the positive effect is the "warranty". (ITIL Concepts) [ITIL Concepts]

24. D - Assessments are useful in the planning, implementation, and measurement phases. (ITIL Concepts) [ITIL Concepts]

25. A - As Service Requests are classified as interruptions which do not reflect a failure in the IT infrastructure, the user whose application caused an error would be the correct response. (Service Management Practices) [Service Management Practices]

26. D - To be most effective, the Change Control process must be impartial to all groups within an organization. This impartiality allows the Change Control team to make decisions that best support the organization as a whole. (Service Management Practices) [Service Management Practices]

27. C - Even if the integrity of measurement data is questionable, it is better than not having any data at all. At the very least, there will be data to question. (General Management Practices) [General Management Practices]

28. B - The Service Catalogue Manager performs the activities above, and also agrees to and documents services, and ensures that information is in alignment with business processes. (Service Management Practices) [Service Management Practices]

29. C - Availability Management is the process responsible for defining,

ITIL Foundation Mock Exam (LITE) 6 - Answer Key and Explanations

analyzing, planning, measuring, and improving all aspects of the Availability of IT services, ensuring that all infrastructure, processes, tools, and other resources are appropriate for the agreed upon SLA targets for availability. (Service Management Practices) [Service Management Practices]

30. D - Both statements above are true. As more demand is generated for services, there is more reason to keep those services maintained. The cost of offering a service to a customer can be recovered from the customer. (General Management Practices) [General Management Practices]

31. A - A process is defined as a structured set of activities designed to accomplish a defined objective. A procedure is a specified way to carry out a process. A work instruction defines how an activity within a procedure should be carried out. (ITIL Concepts) [ITIL Concepts]

32. D - The Service Desk offers the highest rate of First-Call Resolution for users' requests for support. Service Desks are generally staffed by agents with a wide range of communication and technical skills to best respond to various types requests for service. (ITIL Concepts) [ITIL Concepts]

33. D - Deming developed a step-by-step improvement approach called the Plan-do-Check-Act Cycle (P-D-C-A). (Generic Concepts and Definitions) [Generic Concepts and Definitions]

34. C - good Practice has already evolved from Best Practice, and is considered to be proven and successful. (Generic Concepts) [Generic Concepts and Definitions]

35. A - Information Security Management must maintain a balance between Prevention, Detection and Correction. (General Management Practices) [General Management Practices]

36. D - The generic sequence of events in the ITIL Process Model is for data to enter, be processed, output, and finally measured. (ITIL Concepts) [ITIL Concepts]

37. B - The Service Desk is the practice which acts as a single point of contact for IT users on a day to day basis. (Service Management Practices) [Service Management Practices]

38. C - The Service Catalog Manager is responsible for the production and maintenance of the Service Catalog, as well as ensuring that information is consistent with the information in the Portfolio. (Service Management

Practices) [Service Management Practices]

39. A - Both of the statements are true. (ITIL Concepts) [ITIL Concepts]

40. B - A Service Improvement Plan (SIP) is the formal plan used to implement improvements to an IT Service; and is a result of the Continual Improvement Practice. (ITIL Concepts) [ITIL Concepts]

ITIL Foundation Mock Exam (LITE) - 7

Test Name: ITIL Foundation Mock Exam (LITE) - 7
Total Questions: 40
Correct Answers Needed to Pass: 30 (75.00%)
Time Allowed: 60 Minutes

Test Description

This is the seventh cumulative ITIL Foundation test which can be used as an indicator for overall performance. This practice test includes questions from key ITIL areas.

Test Questions

1. Under Continual Improvement, what types of metrics are typically associated with system components, application performance, and availability?

   A. Baseline Metrics

   B. Service Metrics

   C. Process Metrics

   D. Technology Metrics

2. The Information Security Management Practice is successfully implemented in an organization when which of the following statements are true: I) Information is available as and when needed II) Information is secured with appropriate level of confidentiality III) Information is complete, accurate and is protected from unauthorized access IV) Information is exchanged between the organization and others in a trusted, authenticated and reliable way.

   A. All of the statements are true

   B. I, II and IV

   C. II, III and IV

   D. I, II and III

3. Under ITIL, the organization or entity responsible for the delivery of a service to a customer is known as what?

   A. Internal Market Team

   B. Supplier

   C. Vendor

   D. Service Provider

4. Service Pipeline, Service Catalog, and Retired Services are defined in which of the following?

   A. Service Request Management

   B. Service Design

   C. Portfolio Management

   D. CMDB

5. Which of the following statements is FALSE with respect to the value provided by the Monitoring and Event Management Practice to the business?

   A. The Monitoring and Event Management Practice cannot help in real-time monitoring to reduce downtime.

   B. The Monitoring and Event Management Practice provides a basis for automated operations.

   C. The Monitoring and Event Management Practice helps detect incidents at a very early stage.

   D. The Monitoring and Event Management Practice can help signal status changes that allow appropriate action to take place by manual intervention.

6. Testing of a new service takes place during the _____ Practice?

   A. Service Design

   B. Deployment Management Practice

   C. Service Validation and Testing Practice

   D. Change Control

7. Echo Systems has setup databases and tools to capture facts and statistics about its IT services. Which of the following cannot be captured this way?

   A. Wisdom

   B. Data

   C. Information

   D. Knowledge

8. What statement below best describes the concept of a "Practice" in ITIL?

   A. A set of coordinated activities combining and implementing resources and capabilities in order

ITIL Foundation Mock Exam (LITE) 7 - Practice Questions

to produce an outcome which creates value for the customer or stakeholder.

B. A logical concept referring to people and automated measures that execute an activity.

C. A means of delivering value to customers by facilitating outcomes they want to achieve, without the ownership of specific costs and risks.

D. The activity of planning and regulating a set of activities, with the objective of consistent outcomes.

9. Dan is researching and analyzing his company's assets and the threats and vulnerabilities those assets are facing. What is this type of analysis called?

A. Business Impact Analysis

B. Disaster Recovery Analysis

C. Business Continuity Analysis

D. Risk Assessment

10. The measure of how quickly a service can be restored to normal operating status by its technical team following a failure or interruption is known as what?

A. Maintainability

B. Serviceability

C. Reliability

D. Availability

11. Brian has the ultimate responsibility for ensuring three specific processes are fit for purpose for the entire lifecycle of the service, from initial design through continual improvement. What is Brian's role?

A. Process owner

B. Process practitioner

C. Product manager

D. Service manager

12. Please select the ITIL Practice most important in support of the Continual Improvement Practice:

A. Service Level Management

B. Contract Negotiation

C. Service Catalog Update

D. Post Implementation Review

13. What role may be delegated to the Service Desk and / or IT Service Management resources, to ensure that auto alerts from relevant services are properly defined and executed?

   A. Problem Manager
   B. Alert Manager
   C. Event Manager
   D. Incident Manager

14. Which of the following choices correctly define the term KEDB?

   A. Knowledge Executive Draft Board
   B. Knowledge Error Database
   C. Known Event Database
   D. Known Error Database

15. When should a Configuration Audit take place?

   A. Following the recovery from a disaster.

   B. Before and after major changes to the IT Infrastructure.
   C. After the detection of an unauthorized change.
   D. All of the above

16. Nora is responsible for the operational management of a process. What is Nora's role?

   A. Process manager
   B. Process planner
   C. Process practitioner
   D. Process owner

17. What type of technology allows authorized support groups to take control of a user's desktop from a different physical location?

   A. Remote control tools
   B. Event management tools
   C. Diagnostic utilities
   D. Discovery, Deployment, and Licensing Technologies

ITIL Foundation Mock Exam (LITE) 7 - Practice Questions

18. John is performing a gap analysis to determine if there is an appropriate balance of security measures for each of the ITIL security perspectives. He is using an Information Security Measure Matrix to perform this assessment. However, he must perform another analysis to identify the level of security required to determine the investment needed to protect his organization's assets. What is this assessment called?

A. Risk Assessment

B. Business Impact Analysis

C. Cost-Benefit Analysis

D. Threat Management

19. Mean time between failures (MTBF) is an indication of which service property?

A. Availability

B. Serviceability

C. Reliability

D. Maintainability

20. Which of the following metrics is calculated as a percentage of agreed upon service time minus downtime?

A. Performance

B. Reliability

C. Availability

D. Capacity

21. Cherryvale Logistics offers a number of services to its users. The Finance Department has recently asked for an expansion of the core business hours its database is available. Which practice is responsible for negotiating this change in the level of service?

A. Operations management

B. Service Level Management

C. IT Service Management

D. Business relationship management

22. Under ITIL, what statement below describing a customer is false?

A. A customer cannot be the business itself

B. A customer can also be a user

ITIL Foundation Mock Exam (LITE) 7 - Practice Questions

C. A customer can be anyone who makes use of an IT service to achieve their specific outcomes

D. A customer pays for the service on behalf of the user

23. Which ITIL Practice ensures the elimination of the root cause of a problem causing an outage?

A. Problem Management

B. Incident Management

C. Event Management

D. SLA

24. What should a Service Management tool, which is implemented by an organization, always reference?

A. The Configuration Management System (CMS)

B. The Portfolio

C. The Service Pipeline

D. The Service Catalogue

25. Under Continual Improvement, what type of metrics are computed from component metrics?

A. Process Metrics

B. Baseline Metrics

C. Technology Metrics

D. Service Metrics

26. Failure to take advantage of an opportunity can be a/an _____.

A. Risk

B. Exposure

C. Failure

D. Threat

27. Organizations should maintain a Supplier Policy based on: 1) Impact and Importance; 2) Risk; 3) Cost

A. 2 and 3

B. 1 only

C. 2 only

D. 1, 2, 3

28. Which of the following items is not a recognized Change Type?

   A. Normal

   B. Standard (Pre-authorized)

   C. Planned

   D. Emergency

29. What stage of the Deming Cycle requires the actual implementation of improvements to Services and Service Management Practices?

   A. Act

   B. Check

   C. Plan

   D. Do

30. Great Outdoors Telecom has developed an SLA for a specific level of service for all their customers. What is this SLA called?

   A. Customer-Based SLA

   B. Hierarchical SLA

   C. Multi-Level SLA

   D. Service-Based SLA

31. How quickly an IT component can be restored to an operational state by the internal support staff is known as:

   A. Reliability

   B. Availability

   C. Serviceability

   D. Maintainability

32. Under Continual Improvement, which of the following are objectives of measuring service?   a. To validate decisions made earlier   b. To justify, with factual evidence, that a specific course of action is required   c. To determine where to intervene in case changes or corrective actions are required

   A. C

   B. B

   C. A

   D. All of these responses / All of the above

33. Configuration items (CIs) are collected, stored, managed, updated, analyzed and reviewed in which of the following?

   A. Service Configuration Management system

   B. Service knowledge management system

   C. Configuration records

   D. Configuration management database

34. What concept allows management to better understand a service's quality requirements, and presents both the associated costs and expected benefits?

   A. Business Case

   B. Technical Service Catalogue

   C. Risk Analysis

   D. Service Portfolio

35. Under ITIL, an external third party who is necessary to support the components involved in providing a service is known as what?

   A. Service Provider

   B. A Supplier

   C. Internal Market

   D. Customer

36. Which process balances capacity and performance demands with costs?

   A. Demand Management

   B. Service Management

   C. Service Financial Management

   D. Capacity and Performance Management

37. The SVS is composed of the Guiding Principles, Governance, Service Value Chain, Continual Improvement and _____.

   A. Practices

   B. Partners

   C. Products

   D. Problems

38. Which of the following types of Service Desks has a low first-contact resolution rate by design?

    A. Central Service Desk

    B. Virtual Service Desk

    C. Help Desk

    D. Call Center

39. In which ITIL Practice are new and existing services developed and tested?

    A. Release Management

    B. Service Configuration Management

    C. Deployment Management

    D. Service Design

40. What practice is being conducted by documenting and subsequently updating the configuration of the backup server and tape library that performs backups for a shared IT service?

    A. Service Offering Definition

    B. Service Configuration Management

    C. Change Control

    D. Service Catalog Management

ITIL Foundation
Mock Exam (LITE) - 7
Answer Key and Explanations

1. D - Technology Metrics are typically associated with system components, application performance, and availability. (Technology Management Practices) [Technical Management Practices]

2. A - Information Security Management Practice is successfully implemented in an organization when all the following statements are true. I) Information is available as and when needed II) Information is secured with appropriate level of confidentiality III) Information is complete, accurate and is protected from unauthorized access IV) Information is exchanged between an organization and others in a trusted, authenticated and reliable way. (General Management Practices) [General Management Practices]

3. D - A service provider reflects the organization or entity responsible for the delivery of a service to a customer. (General Management Practices) [General Management Practices]

4. C - A Portfolio includes information on the complete set of services managed by a service provider, and includes the Service Pipeline, the Service Catalog, and Retired Services. (General Management Practices) [General Management Practices]

5. A - The Monitoring and Event Management Practice can help significantly reduce downtime by automating monitoring activity. (Service Management Practices) [Service Management Practices]

6. C - New or enhanced services are tested to ensure proper functionality prior to release during the Service Validation Practice. (Service Management Practices) [Service Management Practices]

7. A - Wisdom comes from having knowledge and experience to make sound judgments and decisions. It is a quality that cannot be captured in a database or tool. (Generic Concepts and Definitions) [Generic Concepts and Definitions]

8. A - ITIL describes a Practice as "A set of coordinated activities combining and implementing resources and capabilities in order to produce an outcome which creates value for the customer or stakeholder." (ITIL Concepts) [ITIL Concepts]

9. D - Risk Assessment is the analysis of the value of assets, identification of threats to those assets, and evaluation

of how vulnerable each asset is to the identified threats. (General Management Practices) [General Management Practices]

10. A - Under Availability Management, the measure of how quickly a service can be restored to normal operating status by its internal technical team following a failure or interruption is known as Maintainability. (Service Management Practices) [Service Management Practices]

11. A - The Process Owner bears the responsibility and accountability for ensuring that a process is fit for purpose for its entire lifecycle. (ITIL Concepts) [ITIL Concepts]

12. A - Service Level Management is the most important practice in support of the Continual Improvement Practice. SLM helps the business and the IT organization understand what needs to be measured and what the results should be. (Service Management Practices) [Service Management Practices]

13. C - The Event Manager is responsible for the activities above, and is typically not identified as a dedicated role; rather, it is played by more than one resource. (Service Management Practices) [Service Management Practices]

14. D - KEDB stands for Known Error Database. (ITIL Concepts) [ITIL Concepts]

15. D - Reviews and audits verify the existence of configuration items, checking that they are correctly recorded in the Configuration Management Database, and that there is conformity between the documented baselines and the actual environment to which they refer. (Service Management Practices) [Service Management Practices]

16. A - The Process Manager is responsible for the operational management of a process, including coordination of the activities required to carry out, monitor, and report on the process. (ITIL Concepts) [ITIL Concepts]

17. A - Remote control tools allow authorized support groups to take control of a user's desktop from a different physical location. (Technical Management Practices) [Technical Management Practices]

18. C - The cost-benefit analysis is used to determine the actual investment in security spending. The cost of reducing or eliminating the threat should not exceed the value of the

asset. (General Management Practices) [General Management Practices]

19. C - The reliability of a service is reported as the mean time between failures (MTBF) or uptime. (ITIL Concepts) [ITIL Concepts]

20. C - Availability is the ability of a service to perform its intended function when required, and is based on its reliability, maintainability, serviceability, and security. (Service Management Practices) [Service Management Practices]

21. B - Service Level Management is the practice responsible for developing, negotiating, monitoring, reporting, and reviewing IT service targets, such as the specific hours a service is guaranteed to be available. (Service Management Practices) [Service Management Practices]

22. A - Under ITIL, a customer can include the business itself which provides the service. As an example, an Accounting department may require a service provided by the IT department, and is charged for it (directly or indirectly). This Practice can sometimes be referred to as "Insourcing". (Generic Concepts and Definitions) [Generic Concepts and Definitions]

23. A - The goal of Problem Management is to minimize the adverse impact of problems on the business that are caused by errors within the IT infrastructure and to prevent the recurrence of incidents related to these errors. (Service Management Practices) [Service Management Practices]

24. B - A Service Management tool which is implemented by an organization should always reference the Portfolio. (Service Management Practices) [Service Management Practices]

25. D - Service Metrics are computed from component metrics, and are the result of the end-to-end service. (ITIL Concepts) [ITIL Concepts]

26. A - Risk Management provides an overall perspective on the level of exposure a situation can experience. (Generic Concepts and Definitions) [Generic Concepts and Definitions]

27. D - Other factors in selecting suppliers would be their willingness to negotiate contract terms to meet the needs of your business. (General Management Practices) [Service Management Practices]

28. C - The three Change Types defined by ITIL are Normal (not pre-approved), Standard (Pre-authorized),

and Emergency. (Service Management Practices) [Service Management Practices]

29. A - The "Act" stage of the Deming Cycle requires implementation of the improvement to the Services and Service Management Practices. (Generic Concepts and Definitions) [Generic Concepts and Definitions]

30. D - Service-Based SLAs cover a service for all clients. Client-Based SLAs are tailored to the specific needs of a single customer. (Service Management Practices) [Service Management Practices]

31. D - Maintainability is the measurement of how quickly and effectively a service can be restored to normal functionality and performance by its internal support staff. (Service Management Practices) [Service Management Practices]

32. D - All of the reasons listed above are valid objectives of Service Measurement. (ITIL Concepts) [ITIL Concepts]

33. A - A Service Configuration Management System is the collection of all tools, databases, and information management systems used to store and manage information on Configuration Items (CIs). A Configuration Management Database (CMDB) is part of the Service Configuration Management System. (Service Management Practices) [Service Management Practices]

34. A - A Business Case presents management with a service's quality requirements and associated delivery costs, in addition to models which outline what a service is expected to achieve. (Generic Concepts and Definitions) [Generic Concepts and Definitions]

35. B - A Supplier is an external third party who provides support to the components involved in delivering a service. (General Management Practices) [General Management Practices]

36. D - The goal of Capacity and Performance Management is to ensure that the current and future capacity and performance demands of the customer regarding IT service provision are delivered against justifiable costs. (Service Management Practices) [Service Management Practices]

37. A - The SVS is composed of the Guiding Principles, Governance, Service Value Chain, Continual Improvement and Practices. (ITIL Concepts) [ITIL Concepts]

38. D - Call Centers are intended to handle and log large volumes of calls, and typically have low resolution rates on the first customer contact. Calls are usually routed to more specialized staff for resolution. (Service Management Practices) [Service Management Practices]

39. D - During the Service Design Practice, an organization designs, develops, and tests new services, as well as modifying and testing existing services. (Service Management Practices) [Service Management Practices]

40. B - The objective of Service Configuration Management is the definition of service and infrastructure components and the maintenance of accurate configuration records. (Service Management Practices) [Service Management Practices]

ITIL Foundation Mock Exam (LITE) - 8

Test Name: ITIL Foundation Mock Exam (LITE) - 8
Total Questions: 40
Correct Answers Needed to Pass: 30 (75.00%)
Time Allowed: 60 Minutes

Test Description

This is the eighth cumulative ITIL Foundation test which can be used as an indicator for overall performance. This practice test includes questions from key ITIL areas.

Test Questions

1. Service Configuration Management is a key process in which ITIL Category of Practices?

    A. General Management

    B. Service Design

    C. Technical Management

    D. Service Management

2. An organization has determined that a service no longer meets minimum functional and technical requirements. Which of the following outcomes should the organization choose for this service?

    A. Refactor

    B. Renew

    C. Retire

    D. Replace

3. The Product/Service Portfolio represents all the resources that are active in the various phases of the _____.

    A. Planning Process

    B. Service Value Stream

    C. Service Strategy

    D. Development Lifecycle

4. A portion of the IT infrastructure which is normally deployed together, and is specified in the organization's release policy, is known as what?

    A. Work Instruction

B. Full Release

C. Release Unit

D. Release Group

5. Nora is responsible for recommending improvements to a service. What role is she filling?

   A. Service Designer

   B. Service Owner

   C. Service Manager

   D. Service Strategist

6. In a number of ways, _____ help create value for stakeholders and are recognized and valued.

   A. Creators

   B. Users

   C. Customers

   D. Services

7. Sonic Industries has implemented a network storage service for the entire organization to use. The cost of this service to each department is determined on a per-megabyte-used basis. However, no actual funds change hands. The costs are used simply for tracking and monitoring purposes, in an effort to encourage efficient use of resources. What is this financial management method called?

   A. Notional Charging

   B. Cost Units

   C. IT Accounting

   D. Indirect Costs

8. Eclipse Systems offers reassurance to its customers that it will meet agreed upon requirements for availability, capacity, continuity, and security. What is this reassurance called?

   A. Rating

   B. Guarantee

   C. Warranty

   D. SLA

9. An online service delivery tracking tool is an example of what type of capability?

   A. Self-help

ITIL Foundation Mock Exam (LITE) 8 - Practice Questions

B. Status reporting

C. Request fulfillment

D. Automated process

10. Which of the following is the measure of average duration between one incident and the next?

   A. Mean Time Between Failure

   B. Mean Time to Restore Service

   C. Restore Time Objective

   D. Restore Point Objective

11. Bill runs the server operations group at Western Associates. The servers this group maintains are considered production devices and are actively providing services to customers. What is the ITIL term for production components?

   A. Managed

   B. Live Environment

   C. Live

   D. Steady State

12. John is a project manager at Wolf Enterprises and is embarking on a product improvement project. He must decide which of two approaches to take to introduce significant changes into the organization. These delivery methods are _____ and _____.

   A. Active and Passive

   B. Waterfall and Agile

   C. Proactive and Reactive

   D. Structured and Unstructured

13. Which of the following statements is TRUE with respect to the definition of a Process?

   A. All processes need not have a process owner.

   B. A process owner and a process manager always are two different roles and two different persons.

   C. A process takes the input and processes the output.

   D. All processes should be measurable, cost and performance driven.

ITIL Foundation Mock Exam (LITE) 8 - Practice Questions

14. Which of the following are the types of change models as per the Change Control Practice?

   A. Normal, Average and Emergency

   B. Standard, Normal and Emergency

   C. Normal, Emergency and Urgent

   D. Standard, Classified and Emergency

15. Which of the following is the aim of Availability Management? I) To identify and resolve any kind of service related Incidents and Problems II)To minimize the duration and impact of Events on IT services to ensure rapid business execution III) To support the effects of Events on services for rapid business operation IV) To examine the Events effected on services for rapid business execution

   A. II only

   B. I only

   C. III only

   D. IV only

16. Improving an organization's efficiency by providing easily accessible and up-to-date information is a function of which process?

   A. Change Management

   B. Configuration Management

   C. Knowledge Management

   D. Service Asset Management

17. To respond to a particular situation or perform a specific task, organizations create service _____ _____.

   A. SLAs

   B. Dimensions

   C. Value streams

   D. Value Chains

18. Which of the following items describes to a customer the services they will be provided, along with the expected level of service, roles and responsibilities?

   A. Availability Management

   B. Service Level Agreement (SLA)

C. Service Design Package

D. Service Catalog

19. Which of the statements below can be considered true / correct? a. An Error Report documents faults or complaints about the service b. A Service Request is an incident which involves a failure in the IT infrastructure

A. B

B. A

C. None of the above

D. All of these responses / All of the above

20. DataMax is releasing a new service to all users in a single operation. What is this release approach called?

A. Automated

B. Big Bang

C. Pull Approach

D. Push Approach

21. A large accounting company has established a stringent Change Control Practice to control the introduction of Changes to the company's IT services and their supporting infrastructure. In which Category is the Change Control process found?

A. Technical Management

B. Service Design

C. General Management Practices

D. Service Management Practices

22. Andy's Rentals acts as a _____ _____, leasing cars for hire. His company hires mechanics and buys cars from American Auto Makers, who act as _____ _____ for Andy's Rentals.

A. Public Service, Private Service

B. Service Provider, Service Consumer

C. Retailer, Wholesaler

D. Customer Service, Consumer Advocate

23. Which of the following statements are TRUE with respect to the Change

Control Practice? I) Respond to business and customer change requests. II) Implement changes as per the agreed SLAs. III) Comply to governance, legal, contractual and regulatory needs. IV) Try to reduce the total number of failed changes by effectively implementing them and therefore reducing service disruption.

A. I and III

B. I, III and IV

C. All of these statements are true

D. I, II, III and IV

24. Justine is developing documentation that includes a cost-benefit analysis of a proposed new service, as well as ramifications of not implementing this new service. What is this type of documentation called?

A. Business Case

B. Risk Management

C. TCO

D. ROI

25. Which of the statements below is not true about the Value Proposition of services?

A. Improving the design of services reduces the risk of variations of customer assets

B. Improving the design of services increases customer performance

C. Service assets provide a source of value, while customer assets act as the recipient

D. Customer assets provide a source of value, while service assets act as the recipient

26. Which two of the following are variants of the Service Catalog? I) User Views II) Customer Views III) IT to IT Service Views IV) Marketing View

A. III and IV

B. I and III

C. I-II-III

D. II and IV

27. There are three types of Change Control. They are Standard, Emergency and _____.

A. Monthly

B. Normal

C. Urgent

D. Regular

28. What is the primary source of demand for services?

A. Incentives

B. Customers

C. Activities

D. Business Processes

29. MaxData has implemented a series of workarounds to keep critical month end batch jobs running as intended. These workarounds do not resolve the problem, rather they allow the business teams to return to work on their month-end reporting tasks as rapidly as possible. What is this Practice called?

A. Incident Management

B. Problem Resolution

C. Problem Management

D. Incident Resolution

30. Which of the following is not an availability measurement perspective?

A. IT Service Provider

B. Technical

C. Business

D. User

31. What ITIL practice keeps track of all the interfaces and dependencies between all present services?

A. Service Management

B. Continual Service Improvement

C. Service Catalogue Management

D. Configuration Management

32. To ensure that a process is continually improved and meets its objectives, it is most critical that the process has which of the following?

- A. Process Capabilities
- B. A Process Policy
- C. A Process Owner
- D. Process Enablers

33. Sonata Hosting offers its customers a basic hosting package, along with several optional supporting services such as additional disk space and static IPs, as well as enhanced service level add-ons offering faster download speeds. What is the comprehensive offering called?

- A. Shared Services
- B. Service Package
- C. Service Provider Pkg
- D. Excitement Factors

34. How does the Service Desk reduce the workload on other IT departments within an organization?

- A. By escalating support calls to second and third-line support only when needed
- B. By intercepting user questions which are easily answered before they reach specialist personnel
- C. By acting as the initial point of contact
- D. All of these responses / All of the above

35. Jennifer is reviewing a document that contains only the services that are currently in operation. What is this document called?

- A. Service Portfolio
- B. Service Menu
- C. Service Listing
- D. Service Catalog

36. Logically related activities within the Service Value Chain, along with who should carry out the activities (i.e. "who does what"), is represented by which term?

- A. Work Instruction
- B. Best Practice
- C. Practice

ITIL Foundation Mock Exam (LITE) 8 - Practice Questions

D. Function

37. The IT management team has developed a Release Policy to govern how all Changes to a specific service are to be implemented. In what ITIL Practice is this policy developed?

   A. Availability Management

   B. Release Management

   C. Change Control

   D. Service Design

38. In ITIL, what is the term used to describe the entity which is responsible for the delivery of a service?

   A. Service Lifecycle

   B. Service Provider

   C. Customer

   D. Market Space

39. What term best reflects a Service Management product's ability to adequately perform?

   A. Continuity

   B. Capacity

   C. Security

   D. Scalability

40. Please state which of the following choices of answers best finishes the statement: "Service Improvements will be possible only if there exists: I) well planned and implemented processes II) performance is monitored on a day-to-day basis III) metrics are gathered appropriately IV) data is gathered systematically"

   A. I, II and III

   B. All of them

   C. I, III and IV

   D. II, III and IV

ITIL Foundation Mock Exam (LITE) - 8 Answer Key and Explanations

1. **D** - Service Management is the correct process. (Service Management Practices) [Service Management Practices]

2. **C** - When a service is deemed to no longer meet minimum technical and functional requirements, it is no longer fit for service and should be retired. In order to be renewed, replaced, or refactored, the service must still meet minimum fitness requirements. (Service Management Practices) [Service Management Practices]

3. **B** - The service portfolio represents the opportunities and readiness of a service provider to serve the customers and the market. (General Management Practices) [General Management Practices]

4. **C** - A Release Unit describes the portion of a service or IT infrastructure that is typically released together, according to the organization's release policy. Depending on the types or items of service asset or service component such as software and hardware, the unit may vary. (Service Management Practices) [Service Management Practices]

5. **B** - The Service Owner bears the responsibility for the initiation, transition, and maintenance of a service, and identifies improvement points for the service he or she owns. (ITIL Concepts) [ITIL Concepts]

6. **D** - Services create value in many ways; some direct and others indirect. It is important that these service provider relationships are identified and valued. (Service Management Practices) [Service Management Practices]

7. **A** - Charging customers for their use of IT Services can be implemented in a number of ways in order to encourage more efficient use of IT resources. Notional Charging is one option, in which the costs of providing Services to customers are communicated but no actual payment is required. (ITIL Concepts) [ITIL Concepts]

8. **C** - Warranty provides the customer a level of reassurance and guarantee to meet agreed requirements. (ITIL Concepts) [ITIL Concepts]

9. **A** - Self-help capabilities allow users to perform frequently requested tasks themselves. These tasks can include online delivery tracking systems, self-

service password changes, and IVR systems that provide account information. These systems reduce the amount of calls received by a Service Desk and increase the efficiency of service delivery. (Service Management Practices) [Service Management Practices]

10. A - Mean Time Between Failure (MTBF) is the average duration between one incident and the next. This is also known as uptime. (ITIL Concept) [ITIL Concepts]

11. C - Live refers to an IT Configuration Item such as a server that is being used to deliver service to customers. A Live Environment is a controlled environment containing Live CI's used to deliver services to customers. (ITIL Concepts) [ITIL Concepts]

12. B - The waterfall delivery method is used when requirements are familiar, and the work is more important than speed. The agile method works best when requirements are uncertain, and speed of delivery is the goal. (ITIL Concepts) [ITIL Concepts]

13. D - All processes should be measurable, cost and performance driven. (ITIL Concepts) [ITIL Concepts]

14. B - The following are the types of change models as per the Change Control Practice: Standard, Normal and Emergency. (Service Management Practices) [Service Management Practices]

15. A - The Aim of the Availability Management Practice is to minimize the duration and impact of Events on IT services to ensure rapid business execution. (Service Management Practices) [Service Management Practices]

16. C - The goal of the Knowledge Management Practice is to provide accessible, quality, and relevant data to an organization's staff, to improve that organization's efficiency. (General Management Practices) [General Management Practices]

17. C - Service Value chain practices respond to Customer requirements. (SVC) [SVC - Service Value Chain]

18. B - The SLA describes to the customer the services they will be provided, along with the expected level of service, roles and responsibilities. (Service Management Practices) [Service Management Practices]

19. B - A Service Request is an Incident which does not involve a failure in the

IT infrastructure. The first statement is correct. (Service Management Practices) [Service Management Practices]

20. B - The deployment of a new or changed service to all users in one single operation is called the Big Bang approach. (Service Management Practices) [Service Management Practices]

21. D - The Service Management Practices are responsible for managing and controlling the introduction of a new or changed service into operation. Configuration Management tools and databases are used to track, among other things, what changed, who approved the change, and when it was changed . (Service Management Practices) [Service Management Practices]

22. B - Andy's Rentals acts as a Server Provider in one transaction and Service Consumer in the second scenario. (Service Management Practices) [Service Management Practices]

23. D - The following statements are TRUE with respect to the Change Control Practices. I). Respond to business and customer change requests on a priority basis. II). Implement Changes as per the agreed SLAs in a cost effective manner. III). Comply to governance, legal, contractual and regulatory needs. IV). Try to reduce the total number of failed changes by effectively implementing them and therefore reducing service disruption. (Service Management Practices) [Service Management Practices]

24. A - A business case provides the justification for the implementation of a new service including the costs, benefits, and risks associated with the new service. (Generic Concepts and Definitions) [Generic Concepts and Definitions]

25. D - Customer assets acts as the recipient of value provided by service assets, so statement B is false. (Generic Concepts and Definitions) [Generic Concepts and Definitions]

26. C - The User View, Customer Views and IT to IT User View are three of the variants of the Service Catalog. (ITIL Concepts) [ITIL Concepts]

27. B - Change Control types are Standard (pre-approved), Emergency (must be implemented immediately) and Normal (executed through planned activities), (Service Management Practices). [Service Management Practices]

ITIL Foundation Mock Exam (LITE) 8 - Answer Key and Explanations

28. D - Business processes are the primary source of demand for IT services. Patterns of business activities (BPA) influence the demand patterns seen by the service providers. (ITIL Concepts) [ITIL Concepts]

29. A - The goal of Incident Management is the restoration of normal service operation as quickly as possible and minimizing the adverse impact on business operations, thus ensuring that the best possible levels of service quality are maintained. (Service Management Practices) [Service Management Practices]

30. B - Measuring availability can be done from three perspectives: business, user, and the IT service provider. (Service Management Practices) [Service Management Practices]

31. C - The purpose of Service Catalogue Management is the development and upkeep of a Service Catalogue that contains all accurate details, the status, possible interactions and mutual dependencies of all present services. (Service Management Practices) [Service Management Practices]

32. C - The Process Owner is responsible for ensuring a process meets its objectives and is continually improved. (ITIL Concepts) [ITIL Concepts]

33. B - A Service Package provides a detailed description of a service to be delivered to customers. The contents include the core service, supporting services, and service level packages. (ITIL Concepts) [ITIL Concepts]

34. D - All of the statements listed are ways the Service Desk reduces the workload on other IT departments within the organization. (Service Management Practices) [Service Management Practices]

35. D - The Service Catalog is a subset of the Portfolio and consists of only active services in operation. The Portfolio represents all active and inactive services in the various phases of their lifecycle. (Service Management Practices) [Service Management Practices]

36. C - In ITIL, a practice describes logically related activities and who should carry them out. (ITIL Concept) [ITIL Concepts]

37. B - The Release Policy sets the release guidelines, constraints, and limits for the organization, and is developed in the Service Management Practices Category of Services. (Service Management Practices) [Service Management Practices]

ITIL Foundation Mock Exam (LITE) 8 - Answer Key and Explanations

38. B - The term "Service Provider" is used to describe the entity which is responsible for the delivery of a service. (ITIL Concepts) [ITIL Concepts]

39. B - This concept is best represented by the term: Capacity. (Service Management Practices) [Service Management Practices]

40. B - Service Improvements will be possible only if there exists I) well planned and implemented processes II) performance is monitored on a day-to-day basis III) metrics are gathered appropriately IV) data is gathered systematically. (Service Management Practices) [Service Management Practices]

Knowledge Area Test: Service Value System (SVS)

Test Name: Knowledge Area Test: Service Value System (SVS)
Total Questions: 20
Correct Answers Needed to Pass: 15 (75.00%)
Time Allowed: 15 Minutes

Test Description

This is a Knowledge Area test focused on the Service Value System (SVS) of ITIL.

Test Questions

1. Which of the following is not one of the four dimensions of ITSM?

   A. Value Streams and Processes

   B. Organizations and People

   C. Partners and Suppliers

   D. Policy

2. The Service Value System (SVS) describes how the five components work together to create value for the enterprise. The components are: Guiding Principles, Governance, Practices, Continual Improvement and _____.

   A. Obtain and Build

   B. Good Practices

   C. Service Value Chain

   D. Best Practices

3. Which of the Guiding Principles of service management advises that all aspects of an organization are considered when providing value in the form of services.

   A. Focus on Value

   B. Design Management

   C. Keep it Simple and practical

   D. Think and work holistically

4. Which Guiding Principle recommends collecting utilization and user feedback data before deciding what can be re-used?

   A. CMS

   B. Optimize and Automate

C. Start Where You Are

D. Design & Transition

5. Governance is a component within the _____.

   A. Four Dimensions of Service Management

   B. Service Value Chain

   C. Guiding Principles

   D. Service Value System

6. Making a recommendation that can guide organizations when adopting service management is defined as a _____.

   A. Guiding Principle

   B. Service Level Agreement

   C. Business Case

   D. Governance

7. Progress Iteratively with Feedback is one of the _____ of governance.

A. Four Dimensions of Service Management

B. Service Value Chain

C. Guiding Principles

D. Contributing Factors of the Four Dimensions of Service Management

8. The central element of the Service Value System is an operating model that outlines the key activities required to respond to demand and facilitate business value through the creation and management of products and services. This element is known as:

   A. Influencing Factors

   B. Service Value Chain

   C. Service Management

   D. Guiding Principles

9. Daniels Manufacturing has a set of formal policies and processes that dictate how its various departments are to operate. They have also documented the roles, responsibilities, and authority of its staff. Together these provide guidance for the management of the business. The

ITIL Practice Test: SVS - Service Value System - Practice Questions development, implementation, and use of this framework is called:

A. Role-based management

B. Operational level agreement

C. Service level agreement

D. Governance

Knowledge Area Quiz: Service Value System (SVS) Answer Key and Explanations

1. D - The four dimensions of IT service management, are: Organizations and People, Partners and Suppliers, Value Streams and Processes, and Information and Technology. (SVS) [SVS - Service Value System]

2. C - The Service Value System (SVS) describes how the five components work together to create value for the enterprise. The components are: Guiding Principles, Governance, Practices, Continual Improvement and Service Value Chain. (SVS) [SVS - Service Value System]

3. D - Think and work holistically is the Guiding Principle of Service Management that ensures that all aspects of an organization are considered when providing service value. (SVS) [SVS - Service Value System]

4. C - The Start where you are guiding principle recommends that services already in place should be measured and/or observed directly to understand their current state and what can be reused. (SVS) [SVS - Service Value System]

5. D - The Service Value System contains Guiding Principles, Governance, Service Value Chain, Practices and Continual Improvement. (SVS) [SVS - Service Value System]

6. A - Guiding Principles can guide an organization in all circumstances. (SVS) [SVS - Service Value System]

7. C - The Guiding Principles include Focus on Value, Start Where you are, Progress iteratively with Feedback, Collaborate and promote visibly, Think and work holistically, Keep it simple and practical and Optimize and automate. (SVS) [SVS - Service Value System]

8. B - An operating model that outlines the key activities to respond to customer demand and facilitate value is the central element of the Service Value System. (SVS) [SVS - Service Value System]

9. D - Governance is the process of defining expectations, granting power, and verifying the performance of an organization or business. (SVS) [SVS - Service Value System]

ITIL Foundation Mock Exam (LITE) - 9

Test Name: ITIL Foundation Mock Exam (LITE) - 9
Total Questions: 40
Correct Answers Needed to Pass: 30 (75.00%)
Time Allowed: 60 Minutes

Test Description

This is the ninth cumulative ITIL Foundation test which can be used as an indicator for overall performance. This practice test includes questions from key ITIL areas.

Test Questions

1. Which of the following statements are TRUE with respect to the SLA? I) The SLA is effectively a service quality level warranty or assurance by the service provider. II) The SLA is considered for each of the services provided by the service provider. III) The success of the SLA determines the quality of the Portfolio and the Service Catalog.

   A. II and III only
   B. I and III only
   C. I and II
   D. None of these statements are true

2. Deepak is the Service Level Manager for a cloud services provider. Which of the following is not one of his responsibilities:

   A. Vendor relationship management
   B. Service Testing
   C. Developing Service Level Agreements
   D. Developing Service Contracts

3. Of the items listed below, which serves as the blueprint for service management products, and specify how service assets interact with customer assets to create value?

   A. Service Catalogue
   B. Service Model
   C. Portfolio
   D. Procedure

4. Capacity and Performance Management Practices fall in the Category of _____ _____.

   A. General Management Practices

   B. Service Design

   C. Service Management Practices

   D. Technical Management Practices

5. SST Logica tracks all of the resources that are active in the various phases of the service. The three main subsets SST Logica relies on are the Service Catalogue, Service Pipeline, and Retired Services. Together, what do these three service subsets represent?

   A. Product/Service Portfolio

   B. Lines of Service

   C. Value

   D. Service Lifecycle

6. Janet has been the Financial Manager at Columbus Furniture Stores. Jim, the IT Director, has requested implementing an activity called _____ to help market the costs of providing technical support. Janet is investigating the possibility of utilizing this tool.

   A. Budgeting

   B. Costing

   C. Accounting

   D. Charging

7. Availability of services, controlling demand, and optimizing the use of existing capacity in a day-to-day service environment are most critical to which of the following categories of ITIL Practices?

   A. General Management Practices

   B. Service Transition Practices

   C. Service Management Practices

   D. Technical Management Practices

8. While aligning IT services with business needs and goals, the service management team at Fairfax Supermarkets reviews the four dimensions of Service Management as they apply to their company. What are these dimensions?

A. Technology, architecture, business practices, customer requirements

B. Teams, infrastructure, processes, policies

C. Priorities, budget, resources, revenue

D. Organization & People, Information & Technology, Partners & Suppliers and Value Streams & Processes

9. The technical support group within an organization is expected to assist with corporate software releases every quarter through specific Release Management activities, as well as ensure the network is consistently accessible via Availability Management activities. What statement below is true?

A. The technical support group is playing multiple roles by performing these activities.

B. The technical support group exists in a functional silo.

C. Because they are a single department, the technical support group is playing a single role regardless of the activities they perform.

D. The technical support group is performing functions outside of its authority.

10. Which of the statements below are true? a. An Event is a notification caused by a deviation in the performance of the infrastructure and is created by a user. b. An Alert is a warning or notice about a change or failure that has occurred, and is controlled by System Management tools and the Event Management Process.

A. A and B

B. A

C. B

D. None of the above area true

11. Which item best reflects a Critical Success Factor in Service Catalog Management?

A. Accurate Service Catalog

B. IT Organization is familiar with the techniques which support the service.

ITIL Foundation Mock Exam (LITE) 9 - Practice Questions

C. Users are familiar with the services delivered

D. All of the above

12. Bayview Bank has received a number of customer complaints about wait times at each of its branches between 11:00 AM and 1:00 PM. Following a detailed analysis of all teller transactions, the bank determined that 30% of customer interactions with tellers are to obtain copies of deposited items and other banking records. To reduce customer wait times to 3 minutes or less, the business team has decided to expand its automated services by providing customers with the ability to retrieve this information from the bank's website as well as from its ATMs. In which ITIL Practice was this decision made?

A. Change Control

B. Relationship Management

C. Business Analysis

D. Strategy Management

13. What are the two main characteristics of Service Assets?

A. Outsourced and rented

B. Shared and Exclusive

C. Internal and External

D. Fit for Use (Warranty) and Fit for purpose (Utility)

14. Acme Systems has contracted with Payroll Pro to handle all their payroll duties. What is type of arrangement called?

A. Business Process Outsourcing

B. Partnership

C. Co-sourcing

D. Shared Services

15. Which of the following service assets does service automation impact the performance of? a. Management b. People c. Product d. Knowledge

A. A and D

B. A and B

C. B, C and D

D. All of these responses / All of the above

ITIL Foundation Mock Exam (LITE) 9 - Practice Questions

16. Status, Root Cause, and Workaround are the main phases of _____

    A. Lifecycle of a Known Error

    B. Incident management

    C. Root Cause analysis

    D. Event management

17. A means of co-creating value is to facilitate the customer's desired outcome. This is known as a _____.

    A. Utility

    B. Value

    C. Warranty

    D. Service

18. A set of connected behaviors or actions which are performed by a person, team, or group in a specific context is known as what?

    A. A Role

    B. A Service

    C. A Resource

    D. An Event

19. Attaining market focus and distinguishing capabilities are objectives of which ITIL Practice?

    A. Continual Improvement

    B. Strategy Management

    C. Portfolio Management

    D. Service Design

20. After a virus outbreak in the main datacenter, the incident response team and senior management of a managed hosting company met to review what went right, what went wrong, and what could be done in the future to prevent occurrences and reduce the amount of time to resolve the problem. What is this review called?

    A. Incident Review

    B. Post-incident Evaluation

    C. Postmortem

    D. Post Implementation Review

21. The Availability Manager is responsible for achieving what level of availability?

    A. Availability equal to or greater than SLA terms

    B. 99.999% uptime during business hours

    C. Availability within +/- 5% of SLA terms.

    D. 100% uptime

22. An engineering team is considered what type of asset?

    A. Capability

    B. Resource

    C. Staff

    D. Human Resources

23. To work out the price for a service, which of the following things must be taken into consideration?

    A. The available market must be considered.

    B. The relevance of the service to the customers must be considered.

    C. All of them

    D. The existing competition for the service must be considered.

24. Big-bang and phased approaches, push and pull approaches, and automated versus manual approaches are all concepts which fall under what Practice?

    A. Availability Management

    B. Release and Deployment Management

    C. Change Management

    D. Service Asset and Configuration Management

25. Why a customer would need a specific service, and subsequently procure that service from a service provider, are drivers behind which of the following?

    A. Warranty

    B. Utility

    C. Value

D. Service Assets

26. What role is responsible for owning, maintaining, and protecting the Known Error Database?

A. Problem Manager

B. Incident Manager

C. Event Manager

D. Alert Manager

27. Which of the following are the key activities within the Service Catalog Management Practice? I) Interfacing with internal support teams and Suppliers and dependencies between IT services and supporting services. II) Agreeing upon a common definition of a service with all relevant parties concerned. III) Interfacing with Portfolio Management to agree upon the contents of the Portfolio and Service Catalog.

A. I and III only

B. I, II and III

C. I and II

D. II and III only

28. What role is responsible for ensuring coordination between the build, test, and release teams; plans service rollouts; and manages the installation of new or upgraded hardware?

A. Asset Manager

B. Service Configuration Manager

C. Change Manager

D. Deployment Manager

29. The Deming Cycle of continual improvement involves which steps?

A. Validation, Verification, Quality Assurance, Independent Analysis

B. Scope, Policies, Reporting, Implementation

C. Design, Pilot, Rollout, Results

D. Plan, Do, Check, Act

30. The security team within a manufacturing corporation has discovered that their web server has been taken offline by a Denial of Service attack. They immediately take the server off the network and conduct an analysis of the source and cause of the attack, followed by a rebuild of the server. What is this Security Management Practice called?

A. Correction

B. Threat Management

C. Correction/ Recovery

D. Detection

31. Goals and requirements should always be _____.

A. RTO

B. SMART

C. RACI

D. PCDA

32. Which of the following are inputs into Capacity and Performance Management Practices?

A. Budgets

B. Business strategies

C. Business requirements

D. All of the above

33. The objective of _____ is to detect events, analyze them and determine the right management action.

A. Exception management

B. Support services

C. Monitoring and Event management

D. Incident management

34. Who is ultimately responsible for ensuring a service meets a client's requirements?

A. Process Owner

B. Upper management

C. Customer Service

D. Service Owner

35. "The ability of an IT service or other CI to perform its agreed function when required is the definition of _____.

A. Maintainability

B. Serviceability

C. Availability

D. Reliability

36. The finance department at Faucets and Fixtures International wants a new accounting application with features that will meet new regulatory mandates for their business. They have asked the IT group to assist with this effort. The IT group analyzes the new application and conducts a study to determine what the resource requirements are for the application, and gathers the specific performance and usage requirements for the finance team. This information is used to determine how large the underlying IT infrastructure such as servers and network gear should be. What is this process called?

A. Continual Improvement

B. Capacity Analysis

C. User Acceptance Testing

D. Application Sizing

37. Which of the following is not one of the three types of metrics tracked by the Continual Improvement Practice?

A. Service Metrics

B. Baseline Metrics

C. Process Metrics

D. Technology Metrics

38. The technical review board at a regional government agency is discussing how a recently discovered email virus could affect their operations, the probability of infection, and mechanisms for reducing the probability or impact. What is this process called?

A. Availability Management

B. Risk Management

C. Systems Management

D. Operations Management

39. Fill in the blank: _____ is the first point of contact for IT service users, and is responsible for processing Incidents and Requests.

A. Help Desk

B. Service Desk

C. Support Staff

D. Service Staff

40. What ITIL Practice is concerned with designing the calculation methods and metrics of services?

   A. Measurement and Reporting

   B. Portfolio Management

   C. Design Management

   D. Architecture Management

ITIL Foundation Mock Exam (LITE) - 9
Answer Key and Explanations

1. C - The following statements are true with respect to the SLA. I) The SLA is effectively a service quality level warranty or assurance by the service provider. II) The SLA is considered for each of the services provided by the service provider. (Service Management Practices) [Service Management Practices]

2. B - Service Level Managers are responsible for developing and managing Service Level Agreements as well as the supporting vendor contracts the service requires. (Service Management Practices) [Service Management Practices]

3. B - A Service Model specifies how service assets interact with customer assets and provides a blueprint for the service management products. (IIL Concepts) [ITIL Concepts]

4. C - Capacity and Performance Practices falls into the Category of Service Management Practices. (Service Management Practices) [Service Management Practices]

5. A - An organization's Service Portfolio is comprised of the Product/Service Catalogue, Pipeline, and Retired Services. (General Management Practices) [General Management Practices]

6. D - Charging is a financial tool where the IT costs are shared by the other company business units. (ITIL Concepts) [ITIL Concepts]

7. C - The Service Management Practices provide guidance on the effectiveness and efficiency for the delivery and support of operational (day-to-day) services to customers, and focuses heavily on the availability of services, controlling demand, and optimizing the use of existing capacity. (Service Management Practices) [Service Management Practices]

8. D - Organization & People, Information & Technology, Partners & Suppliers and Value Streams & Processes are the Four Dimensions of IT Service Management. (ITIL Concepts) [ITIL Concepts]

9. A - A single group within an organization may play several roles, as demonstrated by the activities described. It is not known whether a functional silo exists, or whether proper authority has been granted. (ITIL Concept) [ITIL Concepts]

10. C - An Event is a change of state of a service, CI, or monitoring tool; and not created by a user. (Service Management Practices) [Service Management Practices]

11. D - Critical Success Factors for Service Catalog Management are: accurate Service Catalog, users are familiar with the services delivered, and the IT Organization is familiar with the techniques which support the service. (Service Management Practices) [Service Management Practices]

12. D - During the Strategy Management Practice, the need for services, as well as their relative importance, value, and costs, is determined. (General Management Practices) [General Management Practices]

13. D - The two main characteristics of Service Assets are Fit for Purpose (Utility) and Fit for Use (Warranty). (Generic Concepts and Definitions) [Generic Concepts and Definitions]

14. A - Using a 3rd party to provide and manage one or more of an organization's business processes, such as payroll or logistics, is called Business Process Outsourcing. The management of this arrangement is part of the Supplier Management Practice. (ITIL Concepts) [ITIL Concepts]

15. D - All of the items listed are significantly impacted by service automation. (Generic Concepts and Definitions) [Generic Concepts and Definitions]

16. A - A Known Error Record documents the Lifecycle of a Known Error, including the Status, Root Cause, and Workaround. (ITIL Concepts) [ITIL Concepts]

17. D - Providing services is a means of co-creating customer outcome. (ITIL Concepts) [ITIL Concepts]

18. A - This statement represents the definition of a role. (Generic Concepts and Definitions) [Generic Concepts and Definitions]

19. B - During the Strategy Management Practice, a service provider, whether an organization or a team within an organization, determines its market focus (where and how it will compete), and distinguishes the capabilities and service assets that will assist the company achieve its focus. (General Management Practices) [General Management Practices]

20. D - After every major problem, while memories are still fresh, a review

should be conducted to capture lessons learned. (Service Management Practices) [Service Management Practices]

21. A - The Availability Manager is responsible for achieving levels of availability that meet or exceed business requirements negotiated and documented in the Service Level Agreement. (Service Management Practices) [Service Management Practices]

22. A - Capabilities are assets used to control or coordinate service resources. Generally speaking, capabilities are experience-based intangibles that are developed over time, such as teams, products or knowledge about a service. (ITIL Concepts) [ITIL Concepts]

23. C - To work out the price for a service, all the following things must be taken into consideration: The relevance to the customer, available market and the competition. (Service Management Practices) [Service Management Practices]

24. B - These concepts describe approaches towards the release of service components, and fall under Release Management. (Service Management Practices) [Service Management Practices]

25. C - In order for a service to have value, it must provide the functionality a customer requires (Utility), and in a guaranteed manner (Warranty). (ITIL Concepts) [ITIL Concepts]

26. A - The Problem Manager is responsible for the Known Error Database, and initiates the formal closure of it and all Problem records. (Service Management Practices) [Service Management Practices]

27. B - Key activities within the Service Catalog Management Practice include interfacing with internal support teams and suppliers; agreeing upon a common definition for services with all relevant parties concerned; and interfacing with the Portfolio Management Practice to agree upon the contents of the Portfolio and Service Catalog. (Service Management Practices) [Service Management Practices]

28. D - The Deployment Manager is responsible for the activities above, and manages all aspects of the release process within an organization. (Technical Management Practices) [Technical Management Practices]

29. D - The ITIL Continual Improvement Model is based on Deming's Cycle of continual improvement: Plan, Do,

Check, Act. (Generic Concepts and Definitions) [Generic Concepts and Definitions]

30. A - Information Security is enforced in an organization by the Correct activity. This practice consists of the following steps: Prevention/ Reduction, Detection/ Repressing/ Correction/ Recovery, and Evaluation. (General Management Practices) [General Management Practices]

31. B - SMART is an acronym for Specific, Measurable, Achievable/ Appropriate, Realistic/ Relevant, and Timely/ Timebound. (Generic Concepts and Definitions) [Generic Concepts and Definitions]

32. D - Capacity and Performance Management uses inputs from both business and technical camps to ensure adequate and appropriate performance and capacity of IT services and components. (General Management Practices) [General Management Practices]

33. C - The objective of Monitoring and Event Management is to detect events, analyze them, and determine the right management action. (Service Management Practices) [Service Management Practices]

34. D - The service owner ensures that the service meets the requirements. (ITIL Concepts) [ITIL Concepts]

35. C - Service availability is a result of Availability (when promised), Reliability, Maintainability (internal support), and Serviceability (supplier support). (Service Management Practices) [Service Management Practices]

36. D - Application Sizing determines the hardware or network capacity required to support new or modified applications and the predicted workload. (Technical Management Practices) [Technical Management Practices]

37. B - The three types of metrics tracked by Continual Improvement are Technology, Process, and Service metrics. (ITIL Concept) [ITIL Concepts]

38. B - Risk Management is the process of identifying, assessing, and controlling risks such as viruses, fire, or critical system failure. (ITIL Concepts) [ITIL Concepts]

39. B - A Service Desk is an ITIL Practice with a number of staff members who deal with a variety of service events. It must be the prime contact point for IT users. (Service Management

ITIL Foundation Mock Exam (LITE) 9 - Answer Key and Explanations

Practices) [Service Management Practices]

40. A - The Measurement and Reporting Practice is concerned with designing the calculation methods and metrics of services. (Technical Management Practices) [Technical Management Practices]

Knowledge Area Quiz: Technical Management Practices

Test Name: Knowledge Area Quiz: Technical Management Practices
Total Questions: 10
Correct Answers Needed to Pass: 7 (70.00%)
Time Allowed: 10 Minutes

Test Description

This practice test specifically targets the ITIL concepts related to the Service Lifecycle.

Test Questions

1. What ITIL Practice plays a dual role as the custodian of technical knowledge and expertise, and provides actual resources to support Service Management?

   A. Application Management

   B. Infrastructure and Platform Management

   C. IT Operations Management

   D. Service Desk

2. Planning for, conducting, and providing guidance for a service deployment and the release of all documentation is the responsibility of which role?

   A. Deployment Manager

   B. Release Manager

   C. Change Manager

   D. Change Advisory Board

3. What ITIL Practice manages and maintains the IT infrastructure by managing the physical IT environment and provides operations control and facilities management?

   A. Technical Management Practices

   B. Service Design

   C. Service Desk

   D. Application Management

4. _____ technologies are being used to manage public digital ledgers enabled through cloud-based services.

   A. Blockchain

   B. OPEX

C. Innovative

D. CAPEX

5. In which of the following areas can Service Management be positively impacted by automation? a. Design and modeling b. Service Catalogue c. Classification and routing d. Optimization

   A. B and C

   B. A and B

   C. A, C and D

   D. All of these responses / All of the above

6. MaxStorage has recently reorganized its IT structure and implemented a Technical Management team. This team helps plan, implement, and maintain a stable technical infrastructure to support the organization's business processes. What roles will be included in this team?

   A. Specialist Technical Architects and Designers and Specialist Maintenance and Support Staff

B. CIO and CTO

C. Senior and Line Managers

D. Change Advisory Manager and Service Operation Manager

7. Which of the following statements regarding Service Automation are true? a. Service Automation is limited to serving during a business's normal operating hours b. Service Automation enables the capturing of knowledge related to a service process; beneficial for when employees are no longer a part of the organization

   A. A and B

   B. Both statements are false

   C. B

   D. A

8. Which of the following statements about Service Management tools are true? a. Service Management tools must always reference the Service Portfolio b. Products should be modified to fit the tools

   A. A

   B. B

Knowledge Area Quiz: Technical Management Practices - Practice Questions

C. A and B

D. Both statements are false

9. The success of a Service Management tool is least likely to be dependent on which of the following items?

   A. Process

   B. Perception

   C. Function

   D. People

10. An insurance company offers its customers tools to view their policies and statements, as well as pay their bills on the company's website. What are these types of tools called?

    A. Portal

    B. Self Help

    C. Web-based

    D. Online

Knowledge Area Quiz: Technical Management Practices Answer Key and Explanations

1. B - The Infrastructure and Platform Management Practice plays a dual role as the custodian of technical knowledge and expertise, and provides actual resources to support the Service Management practices. (Technical Management Practices) [Technical Management Practices]

2. A - The Deployment Manager is responsible for the final service implementation, from delegation to wrap-up metric reporting. (Technical Management Practices) [Technical Management Practices]

3. A - The IT infrastructure manages the physical IT environment. (Technical Management Practices) [Technical Management Practices]

4. A - Blockchain technologies are being used to manage public digital ledgers enabled through cloud-based services. (Technical Management Practices) [Technical Management Practices]

5. D - Service Management can benefit from automation in all of the areas listed; in addition, pattern recognition and analysis, and detection and monitoring may also be improved. (Technical Management Practices) [Technical Management Practices]

6. A - It is important that the Technical Management Practices be made up of both support and design staff to ensure that a quality, supportable design is implemented. (Technical Management Practices) [Technical Management Practices]

7. C - A strength of Service Automation is that it can operate outside of normal business hours. (Technical Management Practices) [Technical Management Practices]

8. A - In general, processes should not be modified to fit the tools; rather, tools should be modified to fit the process. Service Management tools should always reference the Portfolio. (Technical Management Practices) [Technical Management Practices]

9. B - The success of a Service Management tool is primarily dependent upon its function. (Technical Management Practices) [Technical Management Practices]

10. B - Self Help tools provide customers with easy access to information and services without the assistance of the organization's staff. Viewing statements and documentation, paying bills, and password resets are

examples of support requests that can be serviced with Self Help tools. (Technical Management Practices) [Technical Management Practices]

Knowledge Area Quiz: Technical Management Practices - Answer Key and Explanations

ITIL Foundation Mock Exam (LITE) - 10

Test Name: ITIL Foundation Mock Exam (LITE) - 10
Total Questions: 40
Correct Answers Needed to Pass: 30 (75.00%)
Time Allowed: 60 Minutes

Test Description

This is the tenth cumulative ITIL Foundation test which can be used as an indicator for overall performance. This practice test includes questions from key ITIL areas.

Test Questions

1. Formulating the organization's goals is the objective of the _____ _____ Practice.

    A. Portfolio Management

    B. Business Analysis

    C. Strategy Management

    D. Project Management

2. Johnson Enterprises' IT Team has determined that an additional storage array will be required to support a new company database. What is this activity called?

    A. Performance Monitoring

    B. Demand Management

    C. Application Sizing

    D. Modeling

3. Under ITIL, what are the Four Dimensions that facilitate effective service provision?

    A. Profit, Procedure, Products, Potential

    B. People, Products, Profit, Performance

    C. People, Procedure, Profit, Planning

    D. Organization & People; Information & Technology; Partners & Suppliers; and Value Streams & Processes

4. What type of technology is used to assist with License Management, and typically requires audit tools which can

be run in an automated fashion from any network location; and is also capable of querying and receiving information on all CIs within the IT infrastructure?

   A. Alerting tools

   B. Discovery, Deployment, and Licensing Technologies

   C. Remote control tools

   D. Service Configuration Management System

5. What is the main purpose of the Service Design Practice?

   A. To design the outputs for the next practice.

   B. To design a service solution for the supplier.

   C. To see that the inputs from the previous stage are delivered properly.

   D. To design new or updated services which will be introduced into the LIVE environment.

6. Which of the following is an example of a Change Control Key Performance Indicator?

   A. Number of Implemented Changes

   B. Number of RFCs Accepted/Rejected

   C. Number of Emergency Changes

   D. All of the above

7. A result for a stakeholder enabled by one or more outputs is the definition of _____.

   A. An outcome

   B. A Value Add

   C. A Service

   D. A goal

8. How quickly can functionality of a service can be restored is a measure of which of the following?

   A. Serviceability

   B. Availability

   C. Reliability

D. Maintainability

9. Maintaining a balance between Prevention, Detection and Correction are the goals of which ITIL Practice?

   A. Availability Management

   B. Information Security Management

   C. Service Continuity Management

   D. Service Validation and Testing

10. As per ITIL 4, which one of the following correctly defines the term Incident?

    A. Any unplanned interruption to an IT Service or reduction in the quality of an IT Service.

    B. Any Event that does not form or constitute the standard operation of an IT Service or causes an interruption to the regular Service there by reducing the quality of Service.

    C. System failure with an unknown root cause.

    D. Payroll System Security log showing many login failure incidents.

11. Service demand can be controlled by which of the following mechanisms?

    A. Physical/ technical constraints and financial constraints

    B. Service Catalog improvements and Business Impact Analysis

    C. Management policies, corporate directives, and dollar cost averaging

    D. Effective IT governance and auditing processes.

12. Select the best terms to fill in the blanks: The _____ is what the customer receives, and the _____ affirms how it will be delivered.

    A. Warranty, Utility

    B. Utility, Warranty

    C. Value, Warranty

    D. Value, Utility

13. Kevin is the Service Desk Manager and is embarking on a process to improve customer service provided by his staff. He consulted Martha, the

ITIL Foundation Mock Exam (LITE) 10 - Practice Questions

Continual Improvement Manager, who suggested he create a seven step practice called the ITIL _____ _____ ____.

A. Support Improvement Initiative

B. Iterative Approach

C. Continual Improvement Model

D. Customer Improvement Practice

14. Which of the following is not a key metric associated with Service Level Management?

A. Customer Satisfaction of SLA Achievements

B. Number of Service Interruptions

C. SLA Targets Missed

D. SLA Breaches in Underpinning Contracts

15. The ongoing maintenance and support of technical components such as mainframes, desktop computers, and databases falls under which ITIL Category of Practices?

A. Service Management Practices

B. General Management

C. Technical Management Practices

D. Monitoring and Event Reporting

16. A baseline helps answer Step 2 of the Continual Improvement Model, which asks: ____ __ ___ _____?

A. Where are we now?

B. How do we get there?

C. Did we get there?

D. What is the Vision?

17. What role is responsible for the sizing and performance testing of new services and systems?

A. Capacity Manager

B. Configuration Manager

C. Service Continuity Manager

D. Availability Manager

18. What role is responsible for negotiating levels of service with the customer through SLAs and supports customer Demands.

A. Service Level Manager

B. Service Request Manager

C. Service Financial Manager

D. Service Catalogue Manager

19. An SLA that governs the availability of a specific application during specific hours for all clients is an example of what type of SLA?

A. Catalog-based SLA

B. Client-based SLA

C. Technical SLA

D. Service-based SLA

20. Of the items listed below, which is least likely to be an example of a Key Performance Indicator for the Service Desk?

A. What was the First-line support resolution rate?

B. What percentage of support calls were functionally escalated within 6 minutes of not being resolved?

C. What was the average time to resolve an incident?

D. What was the number of incidents resulting from changes?

21. Janet manages a Service Desk and is interviewing candidates for customer support representatives. Which of the following is the most important for this role?

A. Technical Skills

B. Industry Knowledge

C. Call Center Application Knowledge

D. Communication Skills

22. The Availability Manager is tasked with ensuring adequate availability of all IT Services. How is adequate availability defined?

A. No outages during core business hours

B. 99.9% availability during core business hours

C. 100% availability

D. Availability matches or exceeds the business requirements

23. Organizational control and governance systems such as SOX or ISO have an impact on the design of _____.

   A. Business organization
   B. Services
   C. Shared services
   D. Measurement systems

24. What is a disadvantage of a Type I Service Provider?

   A. Limited decision rights
   B. Specialized in a limited set of business needs
   C. Growth is tied to the growth of the business unit
   D. Short lines of communication

25. In ITIL 4, there are several modeling sources. Among them are Insourcing, Outsources and _____-_____.

   A. Multi-sourcing
   B. Support-sourcing
   C. Near-Sourcing
   D. Far-Sourcing

26. Measurement and analysis of SLA achievement is a main objective of:

   A. Continuous Improvement Management
   B. The service owner
   C. IT Service management processes
   D. Quality control

27. What generic concept is critical for an IT service to succeed, and must be measured regularly by Key Performance Indicators (KPIs)?

   A. Overhead
   B. Core Value
   C. Service Lifecycle
   D. Critical Success Factor (CSF)

28. Under Continual Improvement, what type of metrics are typically captured

in the form of Key Performance Indicators (KPIs), Critical Success Factors (CSFs) and relate to practices within Service Management?

A. Baseline Metrics

B. Service Metrics

C. Practice Metrics

D. Technology Metrics

29. A change of state of a CI that could have an effect on a service is the definition of an _____.

A. Problem

B. Event

C. Incident

D. Known Error

30. What practice manages the performance and capacity of services and resources, and maintains a Capacity Plan which reflects the current and future needs of the organization?

A. Availability Management

B. Service Level Management

C. Service Catalogue Management

D. Capacity and Performance Management

31. Security policies provide a balance between prevention, detection and _____.

A. Security Management

B. Identity Protection

C. Policy Definition

D. Correction

32. Fill in the blank: _____ and _____ are used to determine priority.

A. Impact and cost

B. Capacity and demand

C. Urgency and impact

D. Urgency and cost

33. What is the benefit of a multi-level SLA?

A. All requirements are captured in a single document.

B. It keeps the SLAs under control and reduces the need for frequent updates.

C. It is generic.

D. It only covers subjects that are relevant to a specific service relating to a specific client.

34. A broad concept reflecting an organization's informed decision making process, underpinned by data from the CMDB and CMS is known as what?

   A. Service Configuration Management Practice

   B. Quality Management System

   C. Service Catalogue

   D. Service Model

35. What statement below best describes the concept of a Service in ITIL?

   A. A set of specialized organizational capabilities for providing value to customers in the form of services.

   B. A team, unit, or person that performs tasks related to a specific process.

   C. A means of enabling value for customers by facilitating outcomes they want to achieve, without the ownership of specific costs and risks.

   D. A logical concept referring to people and automated measures that execute a defined process, an activity, or a combination thereof.

36. Availability management monitors, measures, analyzes, and reports on:

   A. Failure rates, recovery method, policy compliance, and process compliance.

   B. Component function, output, utilization, and mean time between failures.

   C. Availability, reliability, maintainability, and serviceability

   D. Availability, redundancy, manageability, and service effectiveness

37. Fitness for Use is used to explain which of the following concepts?

A. Value

B. Service

C. Utility

D. Warranty

38. IT Asset Management ensures accurate inventory information is available in an _____ _____.

A. CMDB

B. CIR

C. CMS

D. Asset Register

39. What is the difference between a Problem and a Known Error?

A. The cause of a Known Error is under investigation, and a Problem is a Known Error that has been resolved.

B. Known Errors are technology related, while Problems are business related.

C. A Known Error is a Problem with a known root cause and a workaround; while the cause of a Problem is unknown and under investigation.

D. A Known Error has no workaround, while a Problem does.

40. Information Security Management is concerned with the maintenance of what elements of an organization's information assets?

A. Privacy, redundancy, criticality

B. Confidentiality, integrity, availability

C. Encryption, loss prevention, risk management

D. Classification, access, confidentiality

ITIL Foundation
Mock Exam (LITE) - 10
Answer Key and Explanations

1. C - Strategy Management is the ITIL Practice that helps develop the organization's goals and objectives. (General Management Practices) [General Management Practices]

2. C - Application Sizing focuses on determining the hardware or network capacity required to support an application and its predicted usage. (Technical Management Practices) [Technical Management Practices]

3. D - The Four Dimensions of Service Management, as defined by ITIL, are: Organization & People; Information & Technology; Partners & Suppliers; and Value Streams & Processes. (ITIL Concepts) [ITIL Concepts]

4. D - A Service Configuration Management System holds information regarding any and all relevant CIs, along with their related attributes, in a centralized location; and is capable of linking to Incident, Problem, and Change records. (Service Management Practices) [Service Management Practices]

5. D - The purpose of the Service Design Practice is to design a new or changed service to be introduced into the LIVE environment. (Service Management Practices) [Service Management Practices]

6. D - Key Performance indicators provide insight into the effectiveness and efficiency of the Change Control process. The metrics include number and type of RFCs and Changes implemented, as well as percentage of success or unsuccessful changes. (Service Management Practices) [Service Management Practices]

7. A - ITIL categorizes SLAs as either Service-based, Customer-based, or Multi-level. (ITIL Concepts) [ITIL Concepts]

8. D - Maintainability is the measure of how quickly a service can be restored in the event of an outage. It is often reported as mean time to restore service (MTRS) or downtime. (ITIL Concepts) [ITIL Concepts]

9. B - Information Security Management's goals are Prevention, Detection and Correction of threats to the company's data, information and knowledge. (General Management Practices) [General Management Practices]

10. A - ITIL 4 defines an Incident as "An unplanned interruption to an IT

Service or reduction in the quality of an IT Service". (Service Management Practices) [Service Management Practices]

11. A - Physical/ Technical constraints such as bandwidth throttling and session timeouts, and Financial Constraints such as penalties for usage in excess of base levels are methods for controlling demand and usage of services. (ITIL Concepts) [ITIL Concepts]

12. B - Utility is what a customer receives (fitness for purpose) and warrant affirms how it will be delivered (fitness for use). (ITIL Concepts) [ITIL Concepts]

13. C - The Continual Improvement Model determines the answers to the following questions: What is the vision? Where are we now? Where do we want to be? How do we get there? (Take Action) Did we get there? How do we keep the momentum going? (Generic Concepts and Definitions) [Generic Concepts and Definitions]

14. B - Many service interruptions do not cause a breach of the SLA and will be tracked by other practices. (Service Management Practices) [Service Management Practices]

15. C - The Technical Management Category of ITIL Practices is accountable for maintaining the infrastructure and components behind the services being offered and is part of Service Management System. (Technical Management Practices) [Technical Management Practices]

16. A - A baseline helps answer Step 2 of the Continual Improvement Model, which asks: Where are we now? (General Management Practices) [General Management Practices]

17. A - The Capacity Manager is responsible for sizing and performance testing of new services and systems. The term "sizing" alludes to capacity. (Generic Concepts and Definitions) [Generic Concepts and Definitions]

18. A - The Service Level Manager performs the activities above, and also identifies the key stakeholders impacted by service levels. (Service Management Practices) [Service Management Practices]

19. D - Service-based SLAs cover a service for all clients. (Service Management Practices) [Service Management Practices]

20. D - Of the options provided, the number of Incidents resulting from

Changes would more than likely reflect a KPI from the Change Control practice (Service Management Practices) [Service Management Practices]

21. D - Communication is the most important skill for Service Desk staff, as their primary role is to act as the single point of contact between the end users and the service provider. Staff must be able to deal with a wide range of people and situations. (Service Management Practices) [Service Management Practices]

22. D - The Availability Manager seeks to deliver availability that matches or exceeds business requirements. (Service Management Practices) [Service Management Practices]

23. B - Service design is constrained by internal resources such as available staff or funding, and by external drivers such as legislative or regulatory controls the organization is subject to. (Service Management Practices) [Service Management Practices]

24. C - The disadvantage of a Type I Service Provider is limited opportunities for growth, as growth is tied to the growth of the business unit. (ITIL Concepts) [ITIL Concepts]

25. A - Multi-sourcing is one of the common sourcing models in practice today. (General Management Practices) [General Management Practices]

26. A - A main objective of the Continuous Improvement Practice is to measure and analyze Service Level Achievements by comparing them to the requirements in the SLA. (Service Management Practices) [Service Management Practices]

27. D - For an IT service to succeed, one or more Critical Success Factors (CSFs) must be identified and measured by associated Key Performance Indicators (KPIs). (ITIL Concepts) [ITIL Concepts]

28. C - Practice Metrics are captured in the form of Key Performance Indicators (KPIs), Critical Success Factors (CSFs) and relate to practices within Service Management. (ITIL Concepts) [ITIL Concepts]

29. B - An "Event" can be described as a change of state of a CI that could have an effect on a service. (ITIL Concepts) [ITIL Concepts]

30. D - As the name suggests, Capacity and Performance Management manages the performance and capacity of services and resources, and

ITIL Foundation Mock Exam (LITE) 10 - Answer Key and Explanations

maintains a Capacity Plan which reflects the current and future needs of the organization. (Service Management Practices) [Service Management Practices]

31. D - Information Security Management is the process of allowing permitted users to access services, while preventing access by users without appropriate permission. It is a result of prevention, detection and correction. (General Management Practices) [General Management Practices]

32. C - Urgency and impact are used to determine priority. (ITIL Concepts) [ITIL Concepts]

33. B - Multi-level SLAs combine corporate, client, and service level SLAs and diminishes the need for frequent updates. (ITIL Concepts) [ITIL Concepts]

34. A - Service Configuration Management Practice leverages underpinning data stored in the CMDB, which flows through the CMS, to make informed decisions. (Service Management Practices) [Service Management Practices]

35. C - ITIL describes a Service as "A means of enabling value for customers by facilitating outcomes they want to achieve, without the ownership of specific costs and risks." (ITIL Concepts) [ITIL Concepts]

36. C - Availability management monitors, measures, analyzes, and reports on availability, reliability, maintainability, and serviceability. (Service Management Practices) [Service Management Practices]

37. D - Fitness for use describes the concept of "Warranty" .(ITIL Concepts) [ITIL Concepts]

38. D - The Asset Register contains accurate information of the enterprise IT Assets and must be kept up to date. (ITIL Concepts) [ITIL Concepts]

39. C - The root cause of a Known Error has been determined and a workaround has been identified. Problems do not have a known root cause and are under investigation. (Service Management Practices) [Service Management Practices]

40. B - Information Security Management is concerned with protecting the confidentiality, integrity, and availability of an organization's information assets. (General Management Practices) [General Management Practices]

Quick ITIL 4 Exam Quiz (I)

Test Name: Quick ITIL 4 Exam Quiz (I)
Total Questions: 10
Correct Answers Needed to Pass:
7 (70.00%)
Time Allowed: 10 Minutes

Test Description

This practice test is a short quiz covering multiple ITIL subject areas.

Test Questions

1. TDD has four basic steps. What is the first step in TDD?

    A. Verify and validate that the test fails

    B. Write product code and apply the test

    C. Refactor the product code

    D. Write test code that will fail

2. Peter is a project leader for an agile project. He makes sure that his team always has a non-threatening environment when it needs to brainstorm. The use of a non-threatening environment is a…

    A. Facilitation method

    B. Asymmetric method

    C. Capitulation method

    D. Prescriptive method

3. You are leading a scientific research and development project that involves a significant number of risks. Overestimating these risks and over-allocating contingency reserves will render the project financially unviable and hence it is critical to estimates the risks at a reasonable level. Which of the following can prove to be effective in addressing variability risks?

    A. Monte Carlo analysis

    B. Root cause analysis

    C. Mitigating opportunities

    D. Accepting the risk

4. A secure repository which stores the authorized versions of software Configuration Items (CIs) is known as a:

Test: Exam Demonstration - Practice Questions

A. CMDB

B. DSL

C. DHS

D. CAB

5. Meghan, as team leader, wants to design a comfortable, collaborative team space for her agile project. What can she do as a basic guideline?

   A. Have plants, natural lighting, and comfortable seating available

   B. Have yearly, individual performance reviews

   C. Seat by team member function

   D. Minimize team member interaction

6. Within an organization, the Marketing department relies on a web analysis software package to review the performance of email marketing campaigns. The web analysis software package is managed internally by the organization's IT support group, which charges the Marketing department for its services. What cost element best reflects this scenario?

   A. Equipment Cost Unit (ECU)

   B. Organization Cost Unit (OCU)

   C. Software Cost Unit (ACU)

   D. Transfer Cost Unit (TCU)

7. Which of the following is a valid Agile project delivery framework?

   A. Plan Do Check Act (PDCA)

   B. Dynamic Systems Development Method (DSDM)

   C. Define Measure Analyze Design Verify (DMADV)

   D. Precedence Diagraming Method (PDM)

8. You are responsible for designing and a new handheld gadget followed by a mass rollout to the market. The project has been requested as a result of your organization's blue ocean strategy, and if successful, will creating a market for its own. However, there is a high degree of uncertainty around the requirements which can only be uncovered through prototyping. Which of the following approaches is most likely to succeed?

A. Using a predictive approach for both design and rollout.

B. Using a hybrid model; Agile approaches for the design phase followed by a predictive approach for the rollout.

C. Using an Agile approach for both design and rollout.

D. Using a hybrid model; predictive approach for the design phase followed by an Agile approach for the rollout.

9. What are the contents of a Definitive Media Library as suggested by ITIL?

   A. Master copies of all controlled documentation

   B. Licenses of all applications and software

   C. Master copies of all developed software application

   D. All of them

10. You are leading an enterprise-wide project than involves a lot of knowledge work. You and the team are currently determining the ideal project management approach for the project. Which of the following Agile measures for estimating user stories is generally recommended if the external stakeholders interested in project estimates are not well-versed with Agile methods?

    A. Cycle time

    B. Velocity

    C. Story points

    D. Ideal days

Test: Exam Demonstration - Practice Questions

Quick ITIL 4 Exam Quiz (I) Answer Key and Explanations

1. D - The TDD process has four basic steps: 1) Write a test, 2) Verify and validate the test, 3) Write product code and apply the test, 4) Refactor the product code. An example may be that a user has to enter an age value. A good test is to make sure the user data entry is a positive number and not a different type of input, like a letter (i.e., write the test). The programmer would verify that entering a letter instead of a number would cause the program to cause an exception (i.e., v&v the test). The programmer would then write product code that takes user entry for the age value (i.e., write the product code). The programmer would then run the product code and enter correct age values and incorrect age values (i.e., apply the test). If the product code is successful, the programmer would refactor the product code to improve its design. Using these four steps iteratively ensures that programmers think about how a software program might fail first and to build product code that is holistically being tested. This helps produce high quality code. [The Art of Agile Development. James Shore.] [Tools and Techniques: Product Quality]

2. A - As a project leader or scrum master, effective facilitation methods are critical for building a high-performance and motivated team. Facilitation of meetings, discussions, demonstrations, etc., is a constant on an agile project. Some general facilitation methods include: using a small number of people for brainstorming events; hosting events in a non-threatening/comfortable environment; having an agenda that is shared with the group ahead of time; using open-ended questions instead of closed-ended questions; including a diverse representation to gain a broader perspective of the topic. [Agile Retrospectives: Making Good Teams Great. Esther Derby, Diana Larsen, Ken Schwaber.] [Knowledge and Skills]

3. A - Variability risks relate to uncertainty existing about some key characteristic of a planned event or activity or decision. Examples of variability risks include: productivity may be above or below target, the number of errors found during testing may be higher or lower than expected, or unseasonal weather conditions may occur during the construction phase. Variability risks can be addressed using Monte Carlo analysis, with the range of variation reflected in probability distributions, followed by actions to reduce the spread of

possible outcomes. [PMBOK® Guide 6th edition, Page 399] [Project Scope Management]

4. B - The Definitive Software Library (DSL) stores the authorized and definitive versions of all software CIs. [Release Management]

5. A - A warm, welcoming environment that promotes effective communication, innovation, and motivated team members is an important aspect to consider when designing team space. Guidelines for a better agile team space include: collocation of team members; reduction of non-essential noise/distractions; dedicated whiteboard and wall space for information radiators; space for the daily stand-up meeting and other meetings; pairing workstations; and other pleasantries like plants and comfortable furniture. [Agile Retrospectives: Making Good Teams Great. Esther Derby, Diana Larsen, Ken Schwaber.] [Tools and Techniques: Communications]

6. D - Costs related to services provided by another department within the organization are known as a Transfer Cost Unit (TCU). [Financial Management for IT]

7. B - Dynamic Systems Development Method (DSDM) is an Agile project delivery framework. Other choices are not Agile approaches. [Agile Practice Guide, 1st edition, Page 151] [Value-driven Delivery]

8. B - Since the product requirements are not known upfront and can only be discovered through a series of prototyping iterations, an Agile approach is suitable for the design phase. Once the product is developed, the mass rollout can be manage using a predictive life cycle. [PMBOK® Guide 6th edition, page 19] [Project Integration Management]

9. D - The contents of a Definitive Media Library as suggested by ITIL are master copies of all applications, Licenses and controlled documentation. (Service Transition) - Selected Processes [ITIL Selected Processes]

10. D - Cycle time and velocity are not user stories sizing measures. In this case, ideal days is recommended because it makes intuitive sense and is easier to explain outside the team. [Cohn, M., 2006. Agile Estimating and Planning. 1st ed. Massachusetts: Pearson Education. Page 72] [Adaptive Planning]

Test: Exam Demonstration - Answer Key and Explanations

ITIL Foundation Mock Exam (LITE) - 11

Test Name: ITIL Foundation Mock Exam (LITE) - 11
Total Questions: 40
Correct Answers Needed to Pass: 30 (75.00%)
Time Allowed: 60 Minutes

Test Description

This is the eleventh cumulative ITIL Foundation test which can be used as an indicator for overall performance. This practice test includes questions from key ITIL areas.

Test Questions

1. The output of Continual Improvement Management planning is a _____.

    A. Critical Success Plan

    B. Improvement Process

    C. Metrics Database

    D. Continual Improvement Plan

2. By organizing work into smaller, manageable sections that can be executed and completed in a timely manner, the focus on each effort will be sharper and easier to maintain is the description of which guiding principle?

    A. Progress iteratively with feedback

    B. Governance

    C. Collaborate and Promote Visibility

    D. Focus on Value

3. Which of the following techniques is used for root cause analysis?

    A. Pareto diagram

    B. Rummler-Brache swim-lane diagram

    C. Kano Model

    D. Ishikawa diagram

4. Value is defined as the combination of which two concepts?

    A. Service Packages and Service Definitions

    B. Warranty and Utility

C. Service Use and Service Design

D. Service Performance and Service Capabilities

5. Information Security Management ensures which elements of an organization's assets, information, data, and services are maintained?

   A. Confidentiality, Integrity, Availability

   B. Baselines, Infrastructure, Processes

   C. Integrity, Confidentiality, and Access Control

   D. Availability, Security, User Rights

6. Which ITIL practice provides a way of comparing the actual performance of a service against its design and SLAs?

   A. Financial Management

   B. Demand Management

   C. Monitoring and Event Management

   D. Capacity and Performance Management

7. Monitoring, measuring, and analyzing the performance of a server with the intent to send an outage alert is which type of activity?

   A. Reliability management

   B. Outage management

   C. Reactive

   D. Proactive

8. Which of the following is not a Continual Improvement metric?

   A. Process Metrics

   B. Logging Metrics

   C. KPIs

   D. Technology Metrics

9. Which practice concerns itself with determining, negotiating, and establishing service delivery target levels.

   A. Service Level Management

ITIL Foundation Mock Exam (LITE) 11 - Practice Questions

B. Capacity and Performance Management

C. Service Continuity Management

D. Availability Management

10. Global Network Services has been contracted to provide maintenance services for a mid-sized manufacturing company. How well Global Network Services meets its contractual obligations is known as which of the following?

A. Availability

B. Reliability

C. Serviceability

D. Maintainability

11. An RFC, a hard drive, an SLA, and an Incident Report are examples of which of the following?

A. Assets

B. Resources

C. Business data

D. Configuration Items

12. In which ITIL Practice Category is the Service Request Management executed?

A. Service Management

B. Continual Improvement

C. Service Transition

D. Service Desk

13. Which ITIL practice is most concerned with disaster recovery planning?

A. Availability Management

B. Risk Management

C. Service Continuity Management

D. Capacity and Performance Management

14. Under Availability Management, what term best describes the measure of how long a service, component, or CI can perform its specific, agreed function without interruption?

A. Reliability

B. Serviceability

C. Availability

D. Maintainability

15. While upgrading their SAN, a large manufacturing conglomerate suffers a server failure. The deployment team immediately initiates the Remediation Plan which includes building new servers with a specific configuration and, later, once service is restored, comparing them to the failed servers in order to learn more about the cause of the outage. What is the specific configuration called?

   A. Backout Baseline

   B. New Growth Baseline

   C. Portfolio Baseline

   D. Configuration Baseline

16. Which of the following ITIL practices relies on practices and methods from Quality Control, Change Management, and the enhancement of capabilities?

   A. Continual Improvement

   B. Service Transition

   C. Service Operation

D. Service Design

17. Which of these tools and methods is appropriate for informing users of scheduled service changes?

   A. Email

   B. Corporate intranet

   C. Verbal communication

   D. All of the above

18. What role assists with Business Impact Analyses by defining the level of control and protection for an organization's information assets; and performs tests which seek to identify information vulnerabilities?

   A. Availability Manager

   B. Service Continuity Manager

   C. Capacity and performance Manager

   D. Information Security Manager

19. Capacity and Performance Management Practices include two

ITIL Foundation Mock Exam (LITE) 11 - Practice Questions

activities: through _____ and _____.

A. Input and Output

B. Improvement and Forecasting

C. Analysis and Planning

D. Service Delivery and Service Support

20. Financial Management Partners' IT group has determined that they will not fix a Known Error in an application used by the HR department. Which of the following is a valid reason for not remediating a Known Error?

A. The costs of the fix may exceed the benefits of fixing the error.

B. The root cause has not been found.

C. The HR division has exceeded its budgeted number of fixes per quarter.

D. The implementation team has not finished its analysis.

21. Fitness for Purpose is used to explain which of the following concepts?

A. Service

B. Warranty

C. Value

D. Utility

22. Which of the following statements are TRUE with respect to Management and Governance? I) Management deals with decision making and process execution. II) Governance deals primarily with decision making and not execution. III) The terms Management and Governance are interchangeable. IV) Management and Governance cannot survive together. Only one of them can be implemented in an organization.

A. III

B. I and II

C. None of the statements are true

D. IV

23. The intangible assets that MaxStorage uses to manage its IT services are known as capabilities. How are these capabilities acquired?

ITIL Foundation Mock Exam (LITE) 11 - Practice Questions

A. Standard procurement processes

B. Capabilities Management Processes

C. They are outsourced

D. They are developed and matured over time

24. What role is responsible for ensuring IT capacity is adequate for the delivery of services, produces and maintains a Capacity Plan, and balances capacity with demand?

A. Availability Manager

B. Demand Manager

C. Service Level Manager

D. Capacity and Performance Manager

25. Which of the following definitions best apply to the Change Models in the Change Control Practice in the Service Management Category?

A. Change Models are templates used in a CMDB which are followed when updating Configuration Items (CIs).

B. Change Models reflect a fixed number and fixed type of steps required to do a change.

C. Change Models are steps to execute a change as defined in the General Management Practice Category.

D. Change Models are defined as pre-established process flows with the necessary steps to satisfy the type of change and level of authorization needed to properly assess the risk and the impact.

26. A Problem whose root cause has already been determined, and for which a Workaround has been documented, is known as what?

A. Alert

B. Incident

C. Known Error

D. Event

27. What term best reflects the uncertainty of an outcome, including negative threats, and positive opportunities?

A. Risk

B. Business Case

C. Procedure

D. Threat

28. Ensuring the confidentiality, integrity, and availability of an organization's IT assets is the goal of which ITIL Practice?

   A. Availability Management

   B. Service Level Management

   C. Information Security Management

   D. Service Continuity Management

29. To be effective, risks need to be: I) Identified, II) Assessed and III) _____.

   A. Treated

   B. Cost effective

   C. Tested

   D. Negative

30. Release types can be categorized into several groups. What type of release is typically implemented as a temporary workaround?

   A. Minor release

   B. Major release

   C. Emergency release

   D. Interim release

31. Which ITIL Practice assures that all goals for a specific service are agreed upon by all responsible parties?

   A. Service Level Management

   B. Service Design Management

   C. Service Value Management

   D. Capacity and Performance Management

32. An addition, modification, or removal of a supported service component to resolve an error found in the service, is known as what?

   A. Change Request

   B. Change

   C. Work Instruction

D. Configuration Item (CI)

33. What term in ITIL best reflects the unknown underlying root cause for one or more incidents?

    A. Event

    B. Service Request

    C. Alert

    D. Problem

34. Which ITIL Category contains the Service Request Management Practice?

    A. Change Control

    B. Continual Improvement

    C. Service Management Practices

    D. IT Asset Management

35. A cloud-based email service provider guarantees in writing that its premier level customers will have access to live support staff 8x7x365. What is this type of documented guarantee called?

    A. Underpinning contract

    B. Service Level agreement

    C. Terms and conditions

    D. Operational level agreement

36. The Configuration Management Practice houses which of the following?

    A. Known Error Database

    B. Supplier and Contract Database

    C. Configuration Management Database

    D. All of the above

37. Which of the following is monitored as part of Continual Improvement Practices?

    A. Performance

    B. Quality

    C. Process compliance

    D. All of the above

38. What generic Service Management term is used to describe technology which allows users to find resolution

to support requests without the assistance of Service Desk personnel, often relying on web based access to accommodate Service Requests?

A. Virtual Service Desk

B. Incident Management System

C. Known Error Database

D. Self-Help technology

D. Service Request

39. What term in ITIL best reflects an unexpected interruption or reduction in the quality of an IT Service?

A. Problem

B. Incident

C. Alert

D. Service Request

40. A pre-approved Change that is low risk and follows a set of procedures, such as creating a new user account, is what type of Change?

A. Standard Change

B. Normal Change

C. Request for Change

ITIL Foundation Mock Exam (LITE) - 11 Answer Key and Explanations

1. D - A Continual Improvement team should measure and report on proposed improvements for services in the Service Catalog and prepare a Service Improvement Plan (SIP). (General Management Practices) [General Management Practices]

2. A - A focus on each effort by organizing work into smaller, manageable sections enables work to be executed and completed in a timely manner. (ITIL Concepts) [ITIL Concepts]

3. D - The Ishikawa Diagram is a technique that helps a team identify all possible causes of a Problem. (Generic Concepts and Definitions) [Generic Concepts and Definitions]

4. B - Value is the combination of Warranty and Utility of the service. (ITIL Concepts) [ITIL Concepts]

5. A - Information Security Management ensures that the confidentiality, integrity, and availability of an organization's assets, information, data, and IT services are maintained. (General Management Practices) [General Management Practices]

6. C - The goal of Monitoring and Event Management is to enable stability in IT Services Delivery and Support by monitoring all events that occur throughout the IT infrastructure to allow for normal service operation and to detect and escalate exceptions. It also provides a way to compare actual performance and behavior against design standards and SLAs. (Service Management Practices) [Service Management Practices]

7. C - Activities that are performed with the intent to address a Problem or Incident after it has already occurred, such as a server outage, are reactive activities. (Service Management Practices) [Service Management Practices]

8. B - Three types of metrics are needed for CSI: technology metrics, process metrics, and service metrics. (General Management Practices) [General Management Practices]

9. A - Service Level Management concerns itself with determining, negotiating, and establishing service delivery target levels. (Service Management Practices) [Service Management Practices]

10. C - The ability of a third-party supplier to meet the terms and

conditions of their contract is known as serviceability. Serviceability is based on how well the supplier meets agreed upon levels of its contract. (ITIL Generic Concepts and Definitions) [Generic Concepts and Definitions]

11. D - A Configuration Item (CI) is any item that supports an IT service. CI's include documents, hardware, software, contracts, and other items necessary for a service offering. (ITIL Concepts) [ITIL Concepts]

12. A - The Service Management Category is concerned with the execution of all strategies, designs, and plans from all areas of service, with primary focus on these processes: Incident Management, Problem Management, Event Management, and IT Access Management. (Service Management Practices) [Service Management Practices]

13. C - Service Continuity Management ensures that the required IT infrastructure and services that support critical business processes can be recovered within required timeframes. (General Management Practices) [General Management Practices]

14. A - Under Availability Management, Reliability describes the measure of how long a service, component, or CI can perform its specific, agreed function without interruption. (Service Management Practices) [Service Management Practices]

15. D - A Configuration Baseline captures both the structure and details of a configuration and is used as a reference point for later comparison. (Service Management Practices) [Service Management Practices]

16. A - Continual Improvement integrates the practices and methods from quality management, Change Control, and the improvement of capabilities. (Service Management Practices) [Service Management Practices]

17. D - Any organizationally appropriate communication method can be used to communicate service changes to users. For some organizations this might be an all hands staff meeting, while other organizations will use an electronic method such as email or text messaging. (ITIL Concepts) [ITIL Concepts]

18. D - The Information Security Manager performs the activities above, and also develops and maintains a Security Policy and Security Plans. (General Management Practices) [General Management Practices]

19. C - Capacity and Performance Management Practices include two activities: through Analysis and Planning. (Service Management Practices) [Service Management Practices]

20. A - Known Errors have a known underlying cause, and a workaround or permanent solution has been identified. However, it may be possible that the cost of the fix outweighs the benefits of fixing the error. (Service Management Practices) [Service Management Practices]

21. D - Fitness for Purpose describes the concept of "Utility". (ITIL Concepts) [ITIL Concepts]

22. B - The following statements are TRUE with respect to Management and Governance. I). Management deals with decision making and process execution. II). Governance deals with only decision making and not execution. (ITIL Concepts) [ITIL Concepts]

23. D - Capabilities of an organization to manage services are intangible assets that cannot be purchased, but instead must be developed and matured over time. (Service Management Practices) [Service Management Practices]

24. D - The Capacity Manager performs the activities above, and also configures capacity monitoring via different types of performance reporting. (Service Management Practices) [Service Management Practices]

25. D - Change Models are pre-established process flows with the necessary steps to satisfy the type of Change and level of authorization needed to properly assess risk and impact. (Service Management Practices) [Service Management Practices]

26. C - A Known Error is a Problem whose cause is known and for which a workaround has been documented. (Service Management Practices) [Service Management Practices]

27. A - A Risk represents an uncertain outcome, and can be positive or negative (opportunity or threat). (Generic Concepts and Definitions) [Generic Concepts and Definitions]

28. C - Information Security Management ensures that the confidentiality, integrity, and availability of an organization's assets, including data, services, and infrastructure, is maintained in accordance with the organization's Guiding Principles.

(General Management Practices) [General Management Practices]

29. A - Risk must be Identified, Assessed and Treated. (General Management Practices) [General Management Practices]

30. C - Emergency releases are usually implemented as a temporary solution for a problem or unknown error. (Service Management Practices) [Service Management Practices]

31. A - Service Level Management assures reliable communication with all responsible parties and maintains the relationships with those parties. It agrees upon the goals of the service provision of these parties and provides the management information required to attain those goals. (Service Management Practices) [Service Management Practices]

32. B - A "Change" best describes the addition, modification, or removal of a service component, to effect corrective actions to resolve errors. (Service Management Practices) [Service Management Practices]

33. D - In ITIL, a Problem is the unknown underlying root cause for one or more incidents. (Service Management Practices) [Service Management Practices]

34. C - Requests by users for support, documentation, information, or other support activities are handled in the Service Management Practice. (Service Management Practices) [Service Management Practices]

35. B - Service level agreements (SLAs) are formally documented guarantees between a service provider and its customer assuring that services will meet targets such as availability, reliability, and/or capacity. SLAs may also define the roles and responsibilities of the customer and/or the service provider. SLAs may be extended to include internal or external customers. (Service Management Practices) [Service Management Practices]

36. D - The Service Configuration Management Practice contains all the tools and databases to manage an IT service provider's configuration data, as well as data on known errors, suppliers, business users, and customers. (Service Management Practices) [Service Management Practices]

37. D - The Continual Improvement Practice monitors and measures the compliance, quality, performance, and business value of a practice. (Service

Management Practices) [Service Management Practices]

38. D - This approach describes the concept of Self-Help technologies. (Technical Management Practices) [Technical Management Practices]

39. B - An incident is an unexpected interruption or reduction in the quality of an IT Service. (ITIL Concepts) [ITIL Concepts]

40. A - A pre-approved Change is low risk, relatively common, and follows a procedure or work instruction. (Service Management Practices) [Service Management Practices]

Quick ITIL 4 Exam Quiz (II)

Test Name: Quick ITIL 4 Exam Quiz (II)
Total Questions: 20
Correct Answers Needed to Pass: 14 (70.00%)
Time Allowed: 20 Minutes

Test Description

This practice test is a short quiz covering multiple ITIL subject areas.

Test Questions

1. What term best reflects a temporary method of resolving an issue, difficulty, or service interruption?

    A. Workaround

    B. Incident

    C. Known Error

    D. Service Request

2. Which of these tools and methods is appropriate for informing users of scheduled service changes?

    A. Email

    B. Corporate intranet

    C. Verbal communication

    D. All of the above

3. Under ITIL, how is the value of a service defined?

    A. Through business outcomes and customer perception

    B. Through revenue and profit generated

    C. Through consistency and quality

    D. Through service cost and demand

4. By organizing work into smaller, manageable sections that can be executed and completed in a timely manner, the focus on each effort will be sharper and easier to maintain is the description of which guiding principle?

    A. Progress iteratively with feedback

    B. Governance

    C. Collaborate and Promote Visibility

    D. Focus on Value

Test: ITIL 4 Exam Demonstration - Practice Questions

5. Any component that helps deliver a product or service is considered to be an __ _____.

   A. IT Asset

   B. Project

   C. Incident

   D. Problem

6. Security policies provide a balance between prevention, detection and _____.

   A. Security Management

   B. Identity Protection

   C. Policy Definition

   D. Correction

7. Which of the following are FALSE with respect to the Change Control Practice? I) Increase the mean time to restore service (MTRS) by quickly and successfully implementing the corrective changes II) Track changes to the service Lifecycle on an on-and-off basis III) Work towards poorer estimations of the quality, time and cost of change IV) Assess the business risks and risks to the customer that are associated with the transition of services

   A. Only III and IV

   B. I, II and IV

   C. I, II and III

   D. All of the statements are false

8. What term best reflects a Service Management product's ability to be substantially enlarged, either via the amount of data it stores, or via the number of users it supports?

   A. Security

   B. Capacity

   C. Scalability

   D. Continuity

9. Service Financial Management is comprised of which three activities?

   A. Budgeting, IT accounting, and demand management

   B. Budgeting, IT accounting, and charging

Test: ITIL 4 Exam Demonstration - Practice Questions

C. Budgeting, analysis, and charging

D. Budgeting, opportunity management, and charging.

10. The IT Asset Manager is responsible for:

   A. Consolidating servers to save money.

   B. Recording the relationships between service assets and configuration items

   C. Full lifecycle management of IT and Service assets from acquisitions to disposal

   D. Configuration auditing

Quick ITIL 4 Exam Quiz (II) Answer Key and Explanations

1. A - A Workaround provides a temporary means of resolving an issue for which an underlying root cause has not yet been resolved. (Generic Concepts and Definitions) [Generic Concepts and Definitions]

2. D - Any organizationally appropriate communication method can be used to communicate service changes to users. For some organizations this might be an all hands staff meeting, while other organizations will use an electronic method such as email or text messaging. (ITIL Concepts) [ITIL Concepts]

3. A - Value is defined by the business outcomes achieved and the customer's perception of that outcome. (ITIL Concepts) [ITIL Concepts]

4. A - A focus on each effort by organizing work into smaller, manageable sections enables work to be executed and completed in a timely manner. (ITIL Concepts) [ITIL Concepts]

5. A - IT Assets are components that are valuable in service or product delivery. (ITIL Concepts) [ITIL Concepts]

6. D - Information Security Management is the process of allowing permitted users to access services, while preventing access by users without appropriate permission. It is a result of prevention, detection and correction. (General Management Practices) [General Management Practices]

7. C - All choices except "Assessing the business risks and risks to the customer that are associated with the transition of services" are FALSE with respect to the Change Control Practice) (Service Management Practices) [Service Management Practices]

8. C - This concept is best represented by the term: Scalability. (General Concepts and Definitions) [Generic Concepts and Definitions]

9. B - Budgeting, IT accounting, and charging are the primary activities performed in Service Financial Management. (General Management Practices) [General Management Practices]

10. C - IT Asset Management is responsible for the management of service assets across the whole lifecycle and maintenance of the asset inventory. (Service Management

Practices) [Service Management Practices]

Knowledge Area Quiz: Selected Processes - Answer Key and Explanations

ITIL Foundation Mock Exam (LITE) - 12

Test Name: ITIL Foundation Mock Exam (LITE) - 12
Total Questions: 40
Correct Answers Needed to Pass: 30 (75.00%)
Time Allowed: 60 Minutes

Test Description

This is the eleventh cumulative ITIL Foundation test which can be used as an indicator for overall performance. This practice test includes questions from key ITIL areas.

Test Questions

1. What are the two types of monitoring tools available for use in the Monitoring and Event Management Practice?

   A. Active and Passive

   B. Primary and Secondary

   C. Software and Hardware

   D. Normal and automated

2. Which Service Management Practice completes regular Business Impact Analyses (BIAs) and ensures services remain available following disasters?

   A. Service Continuity Management

   B. Capacity and Performance Management

   C. Availability Management

   D. Service Level Management

3. Which of the following practices can result in service restoration by a workaround?

   A. Incident management

   B. Systems management

   C. Event management

   D. Problem management

4. The Service Desk is flooded with calls from customers who can no longer work due to a system failure. By further questioning callers, it is apparent that a system-wide update occurred which crashed the central server. For which of the following

activities is the Service Desk not responsible for?

A. Prioritizing the incoming customer calls

B. Escalating the incidents to more specialized personnel

C. Categorizing the incoming customer calls

D. Investigating and identifying the cause of the failure

5. Supporting business continuity by ensuring that required IT facilities can be restored within an agreed time is the focus of:

A. Incident management

B. Service Continuity Management

C. Backup and restore processes

D. Disaster recovery planning

6. Which of the following statements is FALSE when deciding the appropriate level for a release unit within an organization?

A. The level of the Release Unit depends on the size of the organization.

B. The level of the Release Unit depends on the storage available in test and production environment.

C. The level of the Release Unit depends on the time need to implement the change and the resource needed to execute it.

D. The level of the Release Unit depends on the ease and amount of Change.

7. Which of the following are risks associated with Service Catalog Management?

A. An inaccurate Service Catalog

B. Users are not familiar with the services delivered

C. An accurate Service Catalog

D. Users are familiar with the services delivered

8. Transitioning services is heavily dependent on technology. Into which

two ITIL Practices does ITIL divide this technology?

A. Capacity and Performance Management and Change Control

B. Release Management and Deployment Management

C. Service Configuration Management and Service Design

D. Availability Management and Supplier Management

9. Which of the Service Desk performance indicators below would least likely be measured by means of a customer survey?

A. Is the user perception of the company improved based on their experience with the Service Desk?

B. Were users provided guidance which was easy to follow and accurate?

C. What was the percentage of calls answered within 45 seconds of entering the system?

D. Was the support call answered politely?

10. To which of the following would an organization refer in order to determine if it currently offers a service of its own that is comparable to a competitor's service?

A. Service Catalog

B. Service Bulletin

C. Service Warranty

D. Service Pipeline

11. Which of the following represents a means of delivering value to customers by facilitating outcomes the customers want to achieve, without the ownership of specific costs or risks?

A. An asset

B. A value

C. A service

D. A system

12. Services that provide the basic results or outcome customers require are called:

A. Supporting Services

ITIL Foundation Mock Exam (LITE) 12 - Practice Questions

B. Basic Factors

C. Value Services

D. Core Services

13. Solis Enterprises experienced a 45-minute outage on its primary internet connection during core business hours. The network group manually transitioned the company's internet access to a slower speed backup connection until the primary circuit came back online. Which process best describes this response?

   A. Problem Management

   B. Availability Management

   C. Event Management

   D. Incident Management

14. What type of Service Catalogue represents the customer's view and includes relationships to the business units that rely on the IT services?

   A. Business Case

   B. Technical Service Catalogue

   C. Customer or User Service Catalogue

   D. Service Pipeline

15. Jose has established a policy for supplier evaluation and selection. The criteria are based on the Importance and impact, costs and _____ of Supplier Management

   A. Valuation

   B. Sourcing

   C. Risks

   D. Benefits

16. A baseline could be created for which of the following?

   A. Uptime percentage

   B. Software configurations

   C. Bandwidth utilization

   D. All of the above

17. An SLA that states network latency will not exceed 2 milliseconds between 8am and 5pm. Which of the following terms best describe what this SLA is measuring?

ITIL Foundation Mock Exam (LITE) 12 - Practice Questions

A. Reliability

B. Maintainability

C. Resilience

D. Availability

18. What practice is responsible for authorizing users or preventing users from using a Service?

A. Rights Management

B. Information Security Management

C. Verification

D. Auditing

19. Which of the following is an activity of the Service Desk?   a. To function as the first point of contact for the customer   b. To investigate the underlying cause of service interruptions for the customer   c. To determine the root cause of incidents as they occur

A. Item B

B. Item C

C. Item A

D. All of these responses / All of the above

20. What are the three phases of Problem Management? I) Error Control, II) Problem Control, III) Problem Identification

A. II

B. I only

C. II, III

D. III

21. Service Level Management Practices are found within which ITIL Practices Category

A. Service Management Practices

B. Service Design

C. Service Management Practices

D. General Management Practices

22. Which of the statements below is not true regarding IT service strategy?

A. IT strategy supports the business through the design of service solutions

ITIL Foundation Mock Exam (LITE) 12 - Practice Questions

B. IT strategy should dictate business strategy

C. Services are supported to maintain agreed service levels while in operation

D. A continual improvement cycle should be adopted to ensure competitiveness

23. Who is the originator of the "Plan-Do-Check-Act Quality Cycle" for Service Improvements?

   A. Jeroen Bronkhorst

   B. W. Edward Deming

   C. Kaizen

   D. Robert Ishikawa

24. Monitoring technology solutions is the responsibility of _____ ___ _____ Management.

   A. Capacity and Performance Management

   B. Monitoring and Event Management

   C. Infrastructure and Platform Management

   D. Organizational Change Management

25. Resilience measures what property of a service or component?

   A. The business critical elements of the service

   B. The ability to function according to requirements

   C. The ability to withstand failure

   D. The ability to recover from failure

26. Which of the following activities helps a Service Provider achieve his business objectives?

   A. Provide stable services to the customer.

   B. Reacting to customer needs.

   C. Predicting the customer needs through preparation and analysis of customer service usage patterns.

   D. Enabling customer's business objectives.

Practice Exams and Quizzes

27. What term best reflects a Service Management product's ability to recover from a failure?

A. Security

B. Capacity

C. Scalability

D. Continuity

28. John has been named the Configuration Manager for InfoTech Systems. Part of his job is to define the naming convention for Configuration Items. What types of items should he consider as he develops this naming convention?

A. Documentation

B. System config files

C. Batch jobs

D. All of the above

29. Having a practical understanding of the wider organization, business processes and the user community in general is a key aspect of a good _____.

A. Business Process Management Practice

B. Service Desk

C. Help Desk

D. Availability Management Practice

30. The likelihood that a risk will occur, and its possible impact determine _____.

A. The business impact of the change

B. The level of risk involved in the activity.

C. The test plan

D. The recovery plan

31. John is responsible for ensuring that a specific database report required by the Finance Team is aligned with that team's business processes, and that the data returned is formatted in a way that is most useful to the Finance Team. In which of the following roles is John serving?

A. Service Manager

B. Service Owner

C. Process Manager

D. Process Owner

32. Which ITIL Category includes the Service Desk Practice?

   A. Service Management Practice

   B. Products & Services

   C. Technical Management Practice

   D. General Management Practice

33. Monitoring utilization of CPU, disk space and network with the intent to proactively increase the amount of these resources available for use is called:

   A. Capacity and Component Management

   B. IT Asset Management

   C. New Product Introduction

   D. Bottlenecking

34. The Service V Model helps us to achieve which of the following objectives?

A. It helps us to understand the difference between the projected business cost and the actual business costs.

B. It helps us understand the validity of quality measurements for a given service.

C. It helps us to understand the verification and validation test requirements of the service.

D. It helps us to understand the customer requirements better.

35. The complete list of all current customer facing IT services and supporting IT services or available for deployment is contained in the:

   A. Service Catalog

   B. Service Database

   C. Service Pipeline

   D. Service Portfolio

36. Periodically conducting internal audits and verifying employee and process compliance is an activity in which ITIL Practices?

   A. Continual Improvement

B. Service Design

C. Service Desk

D. Service Transition

37. A service package consists of a Service Level Package and one or more:

A. Core Services and Supporting Services

B. SLAs and Warranties

C. Customer Service Packages and Core Services

D. Supporting Services and Enhanced Services

38. Which opportunity analysis tool uses a 4-part table to compare internal and external conditions that could affect the implementation?

A. Waterfall Model

B. SWOT

C. Rummler-Brache Swim Lane Diagram

D. Balanced Score Card

39. What item is responsible for storing information only on those services which are currently active and being offered by the organization?

A. Service Specification

B. Service Catalogue Management

C. Portfolio Management

D. Service Pipeline

40. The phases of the Deming Cycle are:

A. Design Build Test Release

B. Plan Prioritize Predict Prevent

C. Plan Do Check Act

D. Design Build Deploy Support

ITIL Foundation
Mock Exam (LITE) - 12
Answer Key and Explanations

1. A - Active and Passive are the two types of monitoring tools available for use in the Monitoring and Event Management Practice. (Service Management Practices) [Service Management Practices]

2. A - The Business Impact Analyses (BIAs) measures the impact of service unavailability. (Generic Concepts and Definitions) [Generic Concepts and Definitions]

3. A - Incident management is concerned with finding the quickest path to service restoration. The workarounds identified in this process address only the symptoms affecting the user experience. Problem management focuses on the identification of the root cause and development of a resolution to prevent the problem from recurring. (Service Management Practices) [Service Management Practices]

4. D - Problem Management is responsible for identifying the cause of failures, not the Service Desk. (Service Management Practices) [Service Management Practices]

5. B - The ultimate goal of Service Continuity Management is to support Business Continuity by ensuring that the required IT facilities can be restored within the agreed timeframe. (Service Management Practices) [Service Management Practices]

6. A - The size of the organization does not matter when deciding the appropriate level for a Release Unit within an organization. (Service Management Practices) [Service Management Practices]

7. A - Risks associated with Service Catalog Management include inaccurate information in the Service Catalog, acceptance of the Service Catalog and its use in operations processes, and accuracy of information supplied by the business, IT, and Service Portfolios. (Service Management Practices) [Service Management Practices]

8. B - The two types of technology that support transitioning services into the live environment are Release Management and Deployment Management. (Service Management and Technical Management Practices) [Service Management Practices]

9. C - The percentage of calls answered within X number of seconds is a quantitative performance indicator not

normally measured by a customer survey, and is typically tracked in an automated fashion. (Service Management Practices) [Service Management Practices]

10. A - The Service Catalog is the complete listing of currently available services a provider is offering. It is one of the three categories of services in the Service Portfolio. (Service Management Practices) [Service Management Practices]

11. C - A service represents a means of delivering value to customers by facilitating outcomes the customers want to achieve, without the ownership of specific costs or risks. (ITIL Concepts) [ITIL Concepts]

12. D - Core services deliver the basic results to the customer. They represent the value that customers require and for which they are willing to pay. (General Management Practices) [General Management Practices]

13. D - Incident Management addresses the symptoms of an unplanned disruption or outage to restore service operation as quickly as possible. It does not address the root cause of the issue. (Service Management Practices) [Service Management Practices]

14. C - The Customer/User Service Catalogue represents the customer's/user's view and includes relationships to the business units and business processes which support IT services. (Service Management Practices) [Service Management Practices]

15. C - Suppler Management criteria is based on the importance and impact, costs and risks of the prospective vendors. (General Management Practices) [General Management Practices]

16. D - A baseline is a "snapshot in time" used to create a starting point for measuring performance or as a foundation for further development. Infrastructure configurations and performance metrics are both candidates for baseline creation. (Generic Concepts and Definitions) [Generic Concepts and Definitions]

17. D - Availability is the ability of a service or component to perform its required function at a stated instant or over a stated period of time. (Service Management Practices) [Service Management Practices]

18. B - In accordance with the Information Security Policy, users are granted the right to use a service, while simultaneously preventing

access to non-authorized users, thus protecting the confidentiality, integrity, and availability of information and infrastructure. (General Management Practices) [General Management Practices]

19. C - The primary activity of the Service Desk is to act as the first point of contact to the customer. Problem Management is tasked with investigating the root cause of service disruptions. (Service Management Practices) [Service Management Practices]

20. C - The three phases of Problem Management are Problem Identification, Problem Control and Error Control. (ITIL Concepts) [ITIL Concepts]

21. A - Service Level Management is found in the Service Management Practices Category. (Service Management Practices) [Service Management Practices]

22. B - Business strategy should dictate IT strategy; IT strategy should not dictate business strategy. (ITIL Concept) [ITIL Concepts]

23. B - W. Edward Deming is the originator of the "Plan-Do-Check-Act Quality Cycle". Otherwise known as the Deming Cycle. (Generic Concepts and Definitions) [Generic Concepts and Definitions]

24. C - Infrastructure and Platform Management is responsible for monitoring technology solutions. (Technical Management Practices) [Technical Management Practices]

25. C - Resilience is the ability of a service or component to withstand failure. (ITIL Concepts) [ITIL Concepts]

26. C - Predicting customer needs through preparation and analysis of customer service usage patterns is one way a service provider can excel in his job. (Service Management Practices) [Service Management Practices]

27. D - This concept is best represented by the term: Continuity. (Service Management Practices) [Service Management Practices]

28. D - The CMDB contains all types of data and information, including operating system files, hardware information, batch jobs, and operating instructions. As a result, the CMDB naming convention must be flexible enough to handle a variety of data and information types. [Service Management Practices] [Service Management Practices]

29. B - A good Service Desk operation has a practical understanding of the wider organization, business processes and the user community in general. (Service Management Practices) [Service Management Practices]

30. B - The likelihood that the risk will occur, and its possible impact determine the risk category of the Change. In practice, a risk categorization matrix is generally used for this purpose. (ITIL Concepts) [ITIL Concepts]

31. D - The Process Owner is responsible for ensuring a service is fit for its intended purpose, and is held accountable for the output of that process. (ITIL Concepts) [ITIL Concepts]

32. A - Although the Service Desk may play a role in supporting a number of practices, it is part of the Service Management Practice. (Service Management Practices) [Service Management Practices]

33. A - The Capacity and Component Management Practice identifies and manages each component in the IT Infrastructure, monitoring for bottlenecks, under or over utilization of resources, and repositioning or adding additional resources as needed. Examples include upgrading a saturated WAN circuit from DS3 to 10 gigabit optical Ethernet, or routing specific traffic to a relatively underutilized Internet connection. (Service Management Practices) [Service Management Practices]

34. C - The Service V Model helps us to understand the verification and validation test requirements of the service. (Generic Concepts and Definitions) [Generic Concepts and Definitions]

35. A - The Service Catalog is a document or database containing information on all IT services that are live or are available for deployment. It includes both customer facing services as well as supporting services required to deliver the service. The Service Catalog is a component of the Portfolio. (Service Management Practices) [Service Management Practices]

36. A - Periodically conducting internal audits, verifying employee and process compliance activities are part of the Continual Improvement Practice. (General Management Practices) [General Management Practices]

37. A - A service package is a detailed description of an IT service that can be delivered to customers. A service package consists of a Service Level

Package and one or more core services and supporting services. (ITIL Concepts) [ITIL Concepts]

38. B - SWOT identifies strength and weakness (internal conditions), as well as opportunity and threats (external conditions) that may impact an organization's ability to meet its goals. (Generic Concepts and Definitions) [Generic Concepts and Definitions]

39. B - The Service Catalogue consists of services currently being offered. The Service Pipeline consists entirely of services in development. The Service Portfolio consists of services in development, services currently being offered, and services which have been retired. (Service Management Practices) [Service Management Practices]

40. C - The four phases of the Deming Cycle are Plan, Do, Check, and Act. The Deming Cycle is also known as the PDCA Cycle. (Generic Concepts and Definitions) [Generic Concepts and Definitions]

ITIL Foundation Mock Exam (LITE) - 13

Test Name: ITIL Foundation Mock Exam (LITE) - 13
Total Questions: 40
Correct Answers Needed to Pass: 30 (75.00%)
Time Allowed: 60 Minutes

Test Description

This is the eleventh cumulative ITIL Foundation test which can be used as an indicator for overall performance. This practice test includes questions from key ITIL areas.

Test Questions

1. Which of the following roles is responsible for recommending service improvements?

    A. Service owner

    B. Product manager

    C. CSI manager

    D. Process owner

2. The actual deployment of a new or updated service is actively managed by which role?

    A. Service Owner

    B. Deployment Manager

    C. Service Catalog Manager

    D. Configuration Manager

3. Incidents are categorized by what two characteristics?

    A. Urgency and impact

    B. Severity and criticality

    C. Resolution and recovery

    D. Investigation and Diagnosis

4. What statement below best describes the concept of Service Management in ITIL?

    A. A team, unit, or person that performs tasks related to a specific process.

    B. A means of delivering value to customers by facilitating outcomes they want to achieve, without the ownership of specific costs and risks.

C. A set of specialized organizational capabilities for providing value to customers in the form of services.

D. A logical concept referring to people and automated measures that execute a defined process, an activity, or a combination thereof.

5. HostIT INC, an outsourcing provider of website hosting and email management, guarantees 24 X 7 network availability and unlimited server storage for its customers. What term best reflects these guarantees?

A. Utility

B. Warranty

C. Availability

D. Capacity

6. What is the most important objective of Service Design?

A. Accuracy of the SLA

B. The design of new or modified services for introduction into a production environment

C. Development of policies and standards

D. Competing effectively with other organizations

7. The Availability Management practice deals with methods and techniques that help one or more of these: I) Analyze service failure II) Prevent service failure III) Assess service failure

A. I, II and III

B. III only

C. II only

D. I only

8. Two companies have decided it would be in their best interests to jointly create disaster recovery (DR) plans that will allow one company to co-locate their mission critical gear in the data center of the other in the event one of their data centers suffers a disaster-level outage. What is this DR approach called?

A. Gradual Recovery

B. Shared Services

ITIL Foundation Mock Exam (LITE) 13 - Practice Questions

C. Counter Measures

D. Reciprocal Arrangement

9. SST Logica keeps a database with details of all the services supplied to their customers. In addition, this database contains information on the Configuration Items (CIs) each service is reliant upon - items which are not visible to their customers. What is the term for this database?

   A. Business Service Catalogue

   B. Technical Service Catalogue

   C. Product/Service Portfolio

   D. Configuration Management System

10. A new or modified service that is released to all users is known as what type of deployment?

    A. Attended

    B. Automated

    C. Big Bang

    D. Push

11. John is tracking the changing usage of a critical service and has discovered a significant increase in use over the last 2 weeks. He has created a report on these findings for the IT executives, who will evaluate the situation and determine if the issue is a matter of changing business requirements or a capacity issue. In which ITIL Practice is this work conducted?

    A. Service Design

    B. Continual Improvement

    C. Availability Management

    D. Deployment Management

12. Any time a new service is developed, or an existing service is modified, it must be checked against which of the following?

    A. Processes

    B. Service pipeline

    C. Technology architectures

    D. Business requirements

13. In the past 6 months, Retro LLC has recorded over 1000 incidents for their

online music service RetrollaOnline.com. Which of the following sources below may have detected and reported an incident? a. An end user of the service   b. A Service Desk agent   c. A monitoring system   d. Personnel from another IT department

A. A, C, and D

B. A and B

C. A and C

D. All of these responses / All of the above

14. What is the service support interface point between a service and its users?

A. The service desk

B. A web page

C. Customer service department

D. none of the above

15. In order to establish a repository for improvement suggestions, Fred created a _____ _____ _____ and developed the criteria for types and sizes of these suggestions.

A. CMDB

B. CMS

C. Service Configuration Management

D. Continual Improvement Register

16. What are the three strategic categories a service investment could fall into?

A. Transform the Business, Grow the Business, Run the Business

B. Cost Savings, Cost Avoidance, Balance Spending

C. Service Improvement, New Service, Service Retirement

D. Business Process Alignment, Risk Reduction, Business Transformation

17. What type of reporting allows for a summary view of overall IT performance and availability, may provide real time information, and is often related in management reports to customers and users?

A. Alerts

B. Discovery, Deployment, and Licensing Technologies

C. Service Catalogue

D. Dashboards

18. Key Performance Indicators are metrics that provide an objective view of a practice's performance. The number of successful changes implemented in a 6 month period is a measure of which practice?

   A. Availability Management

   B. Service Configuration Management

   C. Capacity and Performance Management

   D. Change Control

19. Before we can embark on an improvement project, it is critical to establish the starting point or _____.

   A. Business Case

   B. Baseline

   C. Project Plan

D. Beginning

20. Understanding why the volume of password related calls is down 25% over the last year is an example of which element of the DIKW structure?

   A. Knowledge

   B. Data

   C. Information

   D. Wisdom

21. A medium sized brokerage firm has hired an outside firm to review its database logs on a regular basis to determine if proper access processes are being followed. During which ITIL Practice would this type of activity occur?

   A. Continual Improvement

   B. Service Management

   C. Risk Management

   D. Information Security Management

22. Fill in the blanks: Utility is to _____ as warranty is to _____.

A. Function, Attributes

B. Profit, Loss

C. Value, Repair

D. Purpose, Insurance

23. Which of the following contain the customer view of IT services?

   A. Business Service Catalog

   B. Technical Service Catalogue

   C. Configuration Catalog

   D. External Service View

24. Which of the following statements regarding an ITIL "practice" is true?

   A. Practices are measurable because they are performance-oriented.

   B. Practices do not respond to a specific event.

   C. Practices are not measurable, because they support functions.

   D. A practice is a specialized subdivision of an organization.

25. Which of the following is an example of an event?

   A. A hard drive reaches its maximum capacity

   B. Firewall failure

   C. Reduction in application response time

   D. All of the above

26. During which ITIL Practices Category are supplier contracts renewed or terminated?

   A. Continual Improvement

   B. General Management

   C. Service Design

   D. Service Management Practices

27. What service principle focuses on the development and refinement of standard IT management processes which lead to services that are available and perform consistently?

   A. Process Management

   B. Stability

ITIL Foundation Mock Exam (LITE) 13 - Practice Questions

C. Cost of Service

D. Responsiveness

28. Fill in the blank: _____ are a necessary condition for a good result in a service or practice/process, and are typically measured by KPIs.

   A. System Metrics

   B. Critical Success Factors

   C. Uptime Factors

   D. Management Input Opportunities

29. What is the proper sequence of the ITIL concepts listed below? a. Good Practice   b. Best Practice   c. Evolution into Commodity, Generally accepted principles, Perceived Wisdom, or Regulatory requirements

   A. B occurs first, C occurs second, A occurs last

   B. B occurs first, A occurs second, C occurs last

   C. A occurs first, B occurs second, C occurs last

   D. A occurs first, C occurs second, B occurs last

30. Which of the following are the goals of the Change Control Practice? I) The Service Configuration Management Practice handles all changes to information on Configuration items and Service assets II) The goal of the Change Control Practice is in alignment with the business goals and all stakeholders' interest   III) To prevent unauthorized changes to the production environment

   A. I and III

   B. I and II

   C. I, II and III

   D. II and III

31. Which role is responsible for ensuring SLA targets for incident resolution are met?

   A. Service Management

   B. Incident Manager

   C. Event Manager

   D. Service Operation Manager

32. A_____ is an unplanned interruption to an IT service, while a (an)_____ is a change to a service component that could cause an interruption to a service.

   A. Technical fault, management fault

   B. Incident, event

   C. Event, incident

   D. Quantities issue, qualitative issue

33. Which of the following is true with respect to the Portfolio? I) The Service Catalog is a subset of the Service Portfolio II) The Service Portfolio is a subset of the Service Catalog

   A. Both I and II

   B. II

   C. I

   D. None of these

34. Rafael has been appointed to head up a project and is creating a project plan. He remembers the last project he served on had used a _____ to help communicate project status, so he added that tool to his project requirements list.

   A. Change Schedule

   B. Daily Newsletters

   C. Kanban Board

   D. Staff Meetings

35. The network infrastructure at a bank branch office is being upgraded to offer increased bandwidth and speed. In the days after the upgrade, the Network Team is onsite to provide support in the event of Problems or Incidents with the new infrastructure. What does ITIL call this type of support?

   A. Early Life Support

   B. Service Management Support

   C. Post Release Support

   D. Service Level Agreement

36. Any component that helps deliver a product or service is considered to be an __ _____.

   A. IT Asset

B. Project

C. Incident

D. Problem

37. Which of the following is not a primary characteristic of products under ITIL?

   A. Products respond to a specific event

   B. Products have specific results

   C. Products are measurable

   D. Products are strategic

38. What practice is made up of nine basic activities, including: planning, building and testing, preparing the deployment, Early Life Support, and reviewing and closing?

   A. Release Management

   B. Change Control

   C. Event Management

   D. Service Validation and Testing

39. Analyzing and tracking patterns of business activities make it possible to do what?

   A. Restrict non-critical activities during peak periods

   B. Prioritize reports and batch jobs

   C. Stagger work start times

   D. Predict demand for services that support the process

40. Connecting Point provides an outsourced Service Desk and call center services for a variety of corporate clients. A report is created at the end of each shift, and the findings are presented at a shift turnover meeting/report, so the incoming staff is aware of issues or incidents that arose during the previous shift. This is an example of what type of policy?

   A. Service Advisory Bulletin

   B. Communication

   C. Change Management

   D. Service Strategy

ITIL Foundation
Mock Exam (LITE) - 13
Answer Key and Explanations

1. A - The Service Owner is responsible for the continual improvement of the services he or she has been assigned. This includes the recommendation of improvement or changes to services as needed. (ITIL Concepts) [ITIL Concepts]

2. B - Deployment Management is actively managed by a Deployment Manager, who is responsible for the daily management and control of the deployment of services or service changes. (General Management Practices) [General Management Practices]

3. A - Incidents are prioritized by impact (the number of resources affected) and urgency (how quickly service can be restored). (ITIL Concepts) [ITIL Concepts]

4. C - ITIL describes Service Management as "A set of specialized organizational capabilities for providing value to customers in the form of services." (ITIL Concepts) [ITIL Concepts]

5. B - The guarantees of Capacity and Availability reflect the concept of Warranty. (ITIL Concepts) [ITIL Concepts]

6. B - According to ITIL, the most important objective of service design is the design of new or modified services for introduction into a production environment. (Service Management Practices) [Service Management Practices]

7. A - Availability Management process deals with methods and techniques that help analyze service failure, prevent service failure and assess service failure. (Service Management Practices) [Service Management Practices]

8. D - Two organizations that plan to utilize the resources of the other in the event of a disaster for one of the organizations have entered into what is called a reciprocal arrangement. (ITIL Concepts) [ITIL Concepts]

9. B - The Technical Service Catalogue encompasses information on services that underpin client services, such as CI relationships. (Service Management Practices) [Service Management Practices]

10. C - Big Bang deployments are used for new or modified services that are rolled out to all users at once. A phased approach impacts only a

specific group or groups of users at a time. (Generic Concepts and Practices) [Generic Concepts and Definitions]

11. B - Continual Improvement is concerned with improving services and processes through constant monitoring, reporting, evaluation, and improvements. (General Management Practices) [General Management Practices]

12. D - An organization must cross check every new and modified service offering against business requirements, to be sure it is fit for its purpose. (General Management Practices) [General Management Practices]

13. D - All response options listed above may have acted as a source for detecting and reporting an Incident. Users detect and report Incidents to the Service Desk. Service Desk agents can detect and directly record Incidents. Monitoring systems are capable of detecting critical events and reporting them to the Incident recording system. Personnel from another IT department may detect an Incident and report it directly to the Incident recording system, or to the Service Desk. (Service Management Practices) [Service Management Practices]

14. A - The Service Desk is the single interface point between a service and its users. Customer service departments and web pages are tools used by the Service Desk to provide assistance to the user base. (Service Management Practices) [Service Management Practices]

15. D - The Continual Improvement Register (CIR) is used as a depository for improvement suggestions. It is an organized list of proposed projects. (Service Management Practices) [Service Management Practices]

16. A - Service investments are split into three strategic categories: Transform the Business, Grow the Business, and Run the Business. (General Management Practices) [General Management Practices]

17. D - Dashboards provide a summary view of overall IT performance and availability, may provide real time information, and are often related in management reports to customers and users. (Generic Concepts and Definitions) [Generic Concepts and Definitions]

18. D - The number of changes implemented is a KPI for Change Control. This metric could be further analyzed to determine the number or percentage of successful changes.

ITIL Foundation Mock Exam (LITE) 13 - Answer Key and Explanations

(Service Management Practices) [Service Management Practices]

19. B - Before we can embark on an improvement project, it is critical to establish the starting point or Baseline. (General Management Practices) [General Management Practices]

20. D - Wisdom comes from knowledge, experience, and judgment. It allows organizations to add value to its services by understanding why specific events happen. (IIL Concepts) [ITIL Concepts]

21. D - This is an Information Security Management ITIL Practice. (General Management Practices) [General Management Practices]

22. B - Utility represents the increase of a possible profit. Warranty represents the decline in possible losses. (ITIL Concepts) [ITIL Concepts]

23. A - The Business Service Catalog contains details of all the IT services delivered to the customer, along with the relationships to the business units and the business processes that rely on the services. (Service Management Practices) [Service Management Practices]

24. A - All practices are measurable, because they are performance-oriented. In addition, practices respond to specific events and have specific results. (ITIL Concepts) [ITIL Concepts]

25. D - All of the above. An event is any change to the state of a Configuration Item that has some significance for the management of that CI. Events include, but are not limited to, total systems failure, a component exceeding its maximum performance threshold, or an item that has changed in a way that could impact service delivery. It is important to note that an Event does not always result in a service interruption. (Service Management Practices) [Service Management Practices]

26. B - Supplier Contract Management are renewed or terminated as an activity of one of the of ITIL General Management Practices Category. (General Management Practices) [General Management Practices]

27. B - Stability focuses on the development and refinement of standard IT management processes which leading to services that are available and perform consistently. (Generic Concepts and Definitions) [Generic Concepts and Definitions]

28. B - A Critical Success Factor is an element that is crucial to an

organization's ability to achieve a specific goal. (Generic Concepts and Definitions) [Generic Concepts and Definitions]

29. B - Under ITIL, Best Practice adoption or development of Best Practice occurs first. Over time the industry will adopt the Best Practice, turning it in to a Good Practice, which will then undergo evolution into a Commodity, Generally accepted principles, Perceived Wisdom, or Regulatory requirements. (Generic Concepts and Definitions) [Generic Concepts and Definitions]

30. C - The following are the goals of the Change Control Practice: I) The Service Configuration Management Practice handles all changes to information on Configuration items and Service assets. II) The goal of the Change Control Practice is in alignment with the business goals and all stakeholders' interest. III) Prevent unauthorized access to make changes to the production environment. (Service Management Practices) [Service Management Practices]

31. B - The Incident Manager is responsible for the management of the Incident Management Team, the effectiveness and efficiency of that team, and meeting or exceeding SLAs for incident resolution. (Service Management Practices) [Service Management Practices]

32. B - An Incident in an unplanned interruption to an IT service, while an Event is a change to a service component that could cause a service interruption. (Service Management Practices) [Service Management Practices]

33. C - The Service Catalog is a subset of the Service Portfolio. (Service Management Practices) [Service Management Practices]

34. C - A Kanban Board is a way to visually communicate the status of activities of a project. Generally, each activity is a line item on the board with a column for the different "states" of the project including "Done". (Generic Concepts and Definitions) [Generic Concepts and Definitions]

35. A - Early Life Support (ELS) is intended to offer additional support and assistance immediately after a service deployment, to ensure any issues are ironed out before a deployment is considered complete. ELS can include onsite support, dedicated phone support, updated knowledge bases, or service

documentation. (ITIL Concepts) [ITIL Concepts]

36. A - IT Assets are components that are valuable in service or product delivery. (ITIL Concepts) [ITIL Concepts]

37. D - Products are not strategic; the providing organization or the customer must know what needs to be achieved. (Service Management Practices) [Service Management Practices]

38. A - These are basic activities of Release Management. (Service Management Practices) [Service Management Practices]

39. D - Business processes are the primary source of demand for services. Patterns of Business Activity influence the demand patterns. The study of these patterns is important for effective Capacity and Performance Management. (ITIL Concepts) [ITIL Concepts]

40. B - Good communication can prevent problems, and every team and department must have a clear communications policy. There are a variety of communication types, including routine operational communication and communication between shifts. (ITIL Concepts) [ITIL Concepts]

ITIL Foundation Mock Exam (LITE) - 14

Test Name: ITIL Foundation Mock Exam (LITE) - 14
Total Questions: 40
Correct Answers Needed to Pass: 30 (75.00%)
Time Allowed: 60 Minutes

Test Description

This is a cumulative ITIL Foundation test which can be used as a baseline for initial performance. This practice test includes questions from all ITIL question categories.

Test Questions

1. Historically, value was provided by a "service provider". In today's highly complex and interdependent service relationships, value is jointly created and referred to as _____ _____. (ITIL Concepts)

    A. Best Practices

    B. Service Management

    C. Good Practices

    D. Value co-creation

2. Which of the following Practices has the ability to identify business priorities and allocate dynamic resources as and when needed?

    A. Problem management

    B. Change Control

    C. Incident Management

    D. Monitoring and Event Management

3. What is a collection of authorized changes to a service called?

    A. Configuration Items

    B. Release

    C. Change Control

    D. Deployment packages

4. Service Level Agreements (SLAs) provide mutually agreed upon terms for various service performance targets. ITIL categorizes SLAs into which three groups?

    A. Service-based, Customer-based, and Multi-level

    B. Service-based, Customer-based, Operations

    C. Service-based, Customer-based, Transaction-based

D. Service-based, Customer-based, Supplier-based

5. The Information Security Practice must maintain a balance between Prevention, Detection and _____.

   A. Correction
   B. Revelation
   C. Resolution
   D. Denial

6. Eastern Enterprises uses password-based access to servers containing employee records. This is an example of using a tool to protect which security tenet?

   A. Availability
   B. Confidentiality
   C. Secrecy
   D. Integrity

7. Your company is planning the future release of a service which will be offered to customers. Where are details regarding the planned service documented? a. Service Pipeline b. Service Catalogue c. Service Portfolio d. Definitive Media Library

   A. A and C
   B. B and C
   C. C and D
   D. A and B

8. Business plans and strategies, Incidents, Problems, SLA breaches, and budgets are inputs into what process?

   A. Continual Improvement
   B. Capacity and Performance Management
   C. Service Level Management
   D. Service Catalog Management

9. An easily quantifiable impact caused by loss of service, such as a loss of revenue, is called a hard impact. A soft impact is less easily quantifiable. Which of the following is an example of a soft impact?

   A. Increase in the cost of delivering services
   B. Increase in facility rent
   C. Shortage of hot spares
   D. Damage to corporate reputation

10. What term best reflects a Service Management product's ability to maintain data integrity?

ITIL Foundation Mock Exam (LITE) 14 - Practice Questions

A. Capacity

B. Continuity

C. Scalability

D. Security

11. What is the most important challenge in Service Catalog Management?

    A. Implementing a Configuration Management System.

    B. Maintaining the Service Knowledge Management System.

    C. Achieving KPIs

    D. Maintaining an accurate Service Catalog.

12. Reviewing progress, fulfillment, effectiveness, and efficiency are key components of what type of review?

    A. Measurement Reporting

    B. Process design

    C. Due care

    D. Process alignment

13. In the Service Management Category of Practices, what practice is comprised of the following four key aspects: Availability, Reliability, Maintainability, and Serviceability?

    A. Service Continuity Management

    B. Supplier Management

    C. Availability Management

    D. Capacity Management

14. Many organizations experience communication difficulties between their technology staff and their internal business units. One way to help alleviate this issue is to create _____ _____ Managers.

    A. Internal Support Teams

    B. Customer Service Representatives

    C. Cross Team Staff Meetings

    D. Business Relationship Managers

15. The executive leadership of Acme Widgets has decided to implement a new CRM platform to provide better service to existing customers and help sales teams identify opportunities based on trending reports. In which ITIL Practice will these goals be defined?

    A. Service Design

    B. Continual Improvement

C. Strategy Management

D. Change Control

16. A Service Desk structure consisting of multiple Service Desks which appear to form a single unit, can be located anywhere, and rely upon modern telecommunication technology is termed:

   A. Virtual Service Desk

   B. Call Center

   C. Centralized Service Desk

   D. Off-shore Service Desk

17. Eastern Enterprises IT division has created a catalog containing the details of the IT services delivered to their customers. This catalog defines the relationships between Eastern Enterprise's business divisions and the processes that are supported by an underlying IT service. What is this catalog called?

   A. Division Service Catalog

   B. Business Service Catalog

   C. Technical Service Catalog

   D. Support Service Catalog

18. An especially dangerous worm has been identified. It has been determined that a security patch must be installed on all vulnerable systems as soon as possible, outside the normal service window for these devices and/or services they support. What is this type of update called?

   A. Proactive change

   B. Risk management

   C. Emergency change

   D. Reactive change

19. The Workforce and Talent Management Practice includes the following activities: Workforce planning, Recruitment, Performance measurement, Learning and development Mentoring and succession planning and _____ _____.

   A. IT Asset Management

   B. Personal Development

   C. Personnel Development

   D. Strategy Management

20. The required security is established by means of policies, processes, behaviors, risk management, and controls, which must maintain a balance between:

   A. Business, Financial, Physical, IT

B. Accounting, HR, Legal, IT

C. Prevention, Detection and Correction

D. Network, Server, Backups, Physical

21. What item below does not represent a primary step in developing a RACI chart?

   A. Identify assignment gaps or overlaps

   B. Review SLA to ensure customer requirements are maintained

   C. Identify the steps involved in the activities

   D. Coordinate meetings to assign RACI codes

22. Service Requirements must be:

   A. RACI

   B. SMART

   C. PDCA

   D. PPPP

23. A successful ITIL implementation requires support at which level of an organization?

   A. Senior management

   B. All levels

   C. Executive

   D. Line workers

24. Which of the following are FALSE with respect to the Change Control Practice? I) Increase the mean time to restore service (MTRS) by quickly and successfully implementing the corrective changes II) Track changes to the service Lifecycle on an on-and-off basis   III) Work towards poorer estimations of the quality, time and cost of change   IV) Assess the business risks and risks to the customer that are associated with the transition of services

   A. only III and IV

   B. I, II and IV

   C. I, II and III

   D. All of the statements are false

25. The ability of an organization to transform resources into services which can offer value to customers is a critical concept for which of the following?

   A. Service Management

   B. Process Model

   C. Good Practice

ITIL Foundation Mock Exam (LITE) 14 - Practice Questions

D. Role

26. The complete set of services offered by a service provider are included in which of the following?

   A. Service Pipeline
   B. Service Catalog
   C. Portfolio
   D. Technology Catalog

27. The four dimensions of Service Management are affected by multiple factors. Organization & People is affected by the _____ factor.

   A. Technological
   B. Political
   C. Legal
   D. Economic

28. A large multinational corporation has outsourced several IT functions to different service providers. Each service provider maintains its own CMS, which is subsequently shared with the customer. This is an example of what?

   A. Organizational strategy
   B. Data integration
   C. Federated CMDB
   D. Multi-sourcing

29. Fill in the blank: The Service Catalog is a subset of the _____.

   A. Portfolio
   B. Service Strategy
   C. Service Pipeline
   D. Service Offering

30. What term is used to describe a significant change of state related to the management of an IT Service or Configuration Item?

   A. Event
   B. Red flag
   C. Alert
   D. RFC

31. Mary Beth is the Release Manager at Stepco Design. She interfaces with the Change Control Team as well as various engineering and infrastructure groups developing new services. Which of the following skills would Mary Beth most need to be successful in this role?

A. Budgeting

B. Public Relations

C. Business Awareness

D. Project Management

32. A measure of achievements of a system, person or team is the definition of _____.

A. Objective

B. Performance

C. A Resource

D. A Deliverable

33. The Service Strategy team are reviewing the requirements for availability, capacity, continuity, and security for a potential new service offering. What key service element do these properties create?

A. Design

B. Utility

C. Value

D. Warranty

34. What is used to measure how well an organization is meeting its goal of reducing calls to the Service Desk for password resets by implementing a self-service tool on the corporate intranet?

A. Patterns of business activities (PBAs)

B. Key performance indicators (KPIs)

C. Critical success factors (CSFs)

D. Operational level agreements (OLAs)

35. What stage of the Deming Cycle requires a comparison of the service improvements which have been implemented, against the metrics of success?

A. Act

B. Check

C. Plan

D. Do

36. Resolving an outage as quickly and efficiently as possible falls within which ITIL Practice?

A. Continual Improvement

B. Problem Management

C. Incident Management

D. Availability Management

ITIL Foundation Mock Exam (LITE) 14 - Practice Questions

37. Your organization has decided to outsource one of its services to a vendor. Which of the following is not considered a risk of outsourcing?

   A. The outsourcing vendor may need to compete with other vendors for your outsourced business

   B. Your organization may become dependent on the outsourcing organization

   C. The outsourcing vendor can end up replacing your organization to the customer

   D. The vendor may damage your organization's reputation

38. What role acts as the primary point of contact to customers for all service related questions and issues, ensures that customer delivery and support requirements are met, and may identify opportunities for service improvements which result in raised RFCs?

   A. Service Owner

   B. Change Manager

   C. Product Owner

   D. Service Level Manager

39. An Incident occurs when:

   A. An employee calls the service desk to report the system for entering work hours is very slow

   B. A Customer Service Rep can't access a needed application

   C. A portion of a network has failed, however it is not noticeable to users because of built in redundancy.

   D. All of the above

40. Kent Industries recently implemented an Employment Benefits Portal for its employees to get information on their individual accounts. Bob Kent recently noticed a drop in access to this tool. He executed an employee survey, which revealed that the tool was frequently unavailable and had not been kept current. He immediately established a plan under the _____ _____ _____ to restore the availability and integrity of the Employee Benefits Portal.

   A. Continual Improvement Practice

   B. Project Management

   C. Availability Management

   D. Relationship Management

ITIL Foundation
Mock Exam (LITE) - 14
Answer Key and Explanations

1. D - Value co-creation is a result of service providers no longer working in isolation, but define value by collaborating with users and customers to determine value. (ITIL Concepts) [ITIL Concepts]

2. C - The Incident management practice has the ability to identify business priorities and allocate dynamic resources as and when needed. (Service Management Practices) [Service Management Practices]

3. B - A group of authorized Changes to a service is called a Release. (ITIL Concepts) [ITIL Concepts]

4. A - ITIL categorizes SLAs as either Service-based, Customer-based, or Multi-level. (ITIL Concepts) [ITIL Concepts]

5. A - The Information Security Practice must contain a balance between Prevention, Detection and Correction. (General Managements Practices) [General Management Practices]

6. B - Protecting information against unauthorized access, by means of tools such as access cards, firewalls, or passwords, ensures the confidentiality of that information. (General Management Practices) [General Management Practices]

7. A - Details on planned services will be documented in the Service Pipeline; The Service Portfolio will contain information on planned, existing, and retired services; hence it will also contain details on the planned service. (Service Management Practices) [Service Management Practices]

8. B - Capacity and Performance Management is critical for ensuring the effective and efficient capacity and performance of services in line with business requirements and overall IT strategic objectives. (Service Management Practices) [Service Management Practices]

9. D - Business Impact Analyses quantify the impact caused by the loss of services. If the impact can be determined in detail, it is called a hard impact. If it is less easily determined, it is called a soft impact. (ITIL Concepts) [ITIL Concepts]

10. D - This concept is best represented by the term: Security. (Generic Concepts and Definitions) [Generic Concepts and Definitions]

11. D - The most important challenge in the Service Catalog Management Practice is maintaining an accurate Service Catalog (containing both the Business and Technical Aspect) as part of the Portfolio. (ITIL Concepts) [ITIL Concepts]

12. A - In order to lead and manage the development process effectively, regular assessments must be

performed. There are four elements that can be investigated: progress, fulfillment, effectiveness, and efficiency. (General Management Practices) [General Management Practices]

13. C - Availability Management is comprised of the following four key aspects: Availability, Reliability, Maintainability, and Serviceability. (Service Management Practices) [Service Management Practices]

14. D - Business Relationship Managers (BRMs) can close the communication gap between technical and business teams. (ITIL Concepts) [ITIL Concepts]

15. C - Strategy Management helps to identify, select, and prioritize new opportunities. (General Management Practices) [General Management Practices]

16. A - A virtual Service Desk appears to users as a single support unit, even though it may consist of many personnel which are remotely dispersed. (Service Management Practices) [Service Management Practices]

17. B - The Business Service Catalog contains details of all the IT services delivered to the customer, together with the relationships to the business units and the business processes that rely on the IT services. This is the customer view of the Service Catalog. (ITIL Concepts) [ITIL Concepts]

18. C - An emergency change is one that takes place as soon as possible, and could be outside the normal change window. Emergency changes are not always critical updates such as security patches. They may also be changes requested to support a project. For example, a development group may need to implement a newly identified firewall rule in a staging environment to permit application testing, and the application schedule will be unacceptably delayed if the team must wait till the next regular change window for the rules to be implemented. (Service Management Practices) [Service Management Practices]

19. B - The Workforce and Talent Management Practice includes the following activities: Workforce planning, Recruitment, Performance measurement, Learning and development Mentoring and succession planning and Personal development. (General Management Practices) [General Management Practices]

20. C - The required security is established by means of policies, processes, behaviors, risk management, and controls, which must maintain a balance between: 1) Prevention: Ensuring that security incidents don't occur; 2) Detection: Rapidly and reliably detecting incidents that can't be prevented; and 3) Correction: Recovering from incidents after they are detected. (General Management

Practices) [General Management Practices]

21. B - Reviewing SLAs does not represent a primary step in the development of a RACI chart. (Generic Concepts and Definitions) [Generic Concepts and Definitions]

22. B - Service Requirements must be SMART: Specific, Measurable, Achievable/ Appropriate, Realistic/ Relevant, and Timely/ Timebound. (Generic Concepts and Definitions) [Generic Concepts and Definitions]

23. B - A successful implementation requires the involvement and commitment of personnel at all levels in the organization. Leaving the development of the practice structures to a specialist department may isolate that department in the organization and it may set a direction that is not accepted by other departments. (ITIL Concepts) [ITIL Concepts]

24. C - All choices except "Assessing the business risks and risks to the customer that are associated with the transition of services" are FALSE with respect to the Change Control Practice) (Service Management Practices) [Service Management Practices]

25. A - The statement describes a core concept of Service Management in ITIL. (ITIL Concepts) [ITIL Concepts]

26. C - The Portfolio contains information on the complete set of services managed and offered by a service provider. The Portfolio includes the Pipeline, the Catalogue, and Retired Services. (General Management Practices) [General Management Practices]

27. B - The Organization and People Dimension of service management is affected by Political Factors. (ITIL Concepts) [ITIL Concepts]

28. C - At the data level it may be that the CMS gets its data from different CMDBs, that together, form a federated CMDB. (Service Management Practices) [Service Management Practices]

29. A - The Portfolio represents the opportunities and readiness of a service provider to serve their customers. The Portfolio is divided into three subsets of activities: The Service Catalog, the Service Pipeline, and Retired Services. (General Management Practices) [General Management Practices]

30. A - An event describes a significant change of state related to the management of an IT Service Configuration Item. An alert is a notification created by an IT service or component indicating an event has occurred. (Service Management Practices) [Service Management Practices]

ITIL Foundation Mock Exam (LITE) 14 - Answer Key and Explanations

31. D - The Release Manager must coordinate tasks, deadlines, and delivery of services and service changes with many different groups within an organization. Of the skills listed, strong project management skills will be most beneficial for this role. (ITIL Concepts) [ITIL Concepts]

32. B - The Performance of a system, person or team is a measure achievement. (Service Management Practices) [Service Management Practices]

33. D - Warranty guarantees the utility of a service by ensuring that it is available and offers sufficient capacity, continuity, and security. (ITIL Concepts) [ITIL Concepts]

34. B - Key performance indicators (KPIs) are used to quantify and measure service elements that contribute to meeting an organization's objectives. In this scenario, reducing the volume of password reset calls is a critical success factor (CSF) that could be measured by a KPI that reports the number and type of calls over time. (ITIL Concepts) [ITIL Concepts]

35. B - The "Check" stage requires a comparison of the service improvements which have been implemented, against the metrics of success. (Generic Concepts and Definitions) [Generic Concepts and Definitions]

36. C - During the Incident Management Practice, an organization delivers and maintains a service to its customer. Minimizing the occurrence, impact, and duration of service outages is an important objective Incident Management. (Service Management Practices) [Service Management Practices]

37. A - Substitution, disruption, and distinctiveness are all risks of outsourcing. Vendor competition is not one of them. (Service Management Practices) [Service Management Practices]

38. A - The Service Owner is responsible for the activities listed above. In addition, the Service Owner will communicate with Product Owners over the course of the lifecycle of the service. (ITIL Concepts) [ITIL Concepts]

39. D - An incident is any unplanned interruption to or reduction in the quality of an IT service. Therefore, all are correct. (Service Management Practices) [Service Management Practices]

40. A - Bob Kent established a plan to review and restore the Kent Industries Employment Benefits Portal and a periodic review of the plan to ensure it remains current. (General Management Practices) [General Management Practices]

ITIL Foundation Mock Exam (LITE) - 15

Test Name: ITIL Foundation Mock Exam (LITE) - 15
Total Questions: 40
Correct Answers Needed to Pass: 30 (75.00%)
Time Allowed: 60 Minutes

Test Description

This is a cumulative ITIL Foundation test which can be used as a baseline for initial performance. This practice test includes questions from all ITIL question categories.

Test Questions

1. What Service Management practice ensures agreed levels of availability defined in the SLA is met, and maintains an Availability Plan which reflects the current and future needs of the organization?

    A. Service Catalogue Management

    B. Service Level Management

    C. Availability Management

    D. Capacity and Performance Management

2. The unknown root cause of an Incident or series of Incidents is referred to as a _____.

    A. Error

    B. Exception

    C. Change

    D. Problem

3. In order to derive meaningful metrics from Continual Improvement, what must be established as a result of the first measurement?

    A. Core value

    B. CSF

    C. KPI

    D. Baseline

4. Johnson Power Controls is conducting a Configuration Audit. Which of the following could be a catalyst for this audit?

    A. Corporate policy requiring audits at regular intervals

    B. Significant changes to the IT infrastructure

    C. Discovery of an unauthorized CI

    D. All of the above

5. Steve is the Service Level Manager of a managed hosting provider. How does he identify and manage improvements to services and processes as part of Continual Improvement?

   A. Conducting quarterly Service Capability Reviews

   B. Constant monitoring, reporting, evaluating, and improving.

   C. Updating the Service Catalog

   D. Delegating authority to the Strategy Management

6. What is the objective of the Service Catalog Management Practice?

   A. To document the Portfolio and ensure its correctness.

   B. To capture metrics that will enable better decision-making and continual improvement of service management practices.

   C. To manage the information within the Service Catalog and to ensure its correctness for implementation in the LIVE environment.

   D. To capture the design of the measurement methods and metrics of the services, as well as the architectures and its processes.

7. Superbrands Stores is rolling out a new pay-per-use Service Desk to supplement the existing web-based self-help system. During the pilot phase, Superbrands departments are alerted to the total charges incurred by their users each week, but no money is actually transferred to cover the cost of the service. This is an example of :

   A. Control Loop Charging

   B. Virtual Charging

   C. Notional Charging

   D. Internal Chargeback's

8. What generic Service Management concept(s) allows defined processes such as an organization's Incident Lifecycle and Change Model to be pre-defined and controlled, resulting in the automatic management of items such as escalation paths and alerting?

   A. Workflow or process engines

   B. Incident workarounds

   C. Service Assets

   D. The Deming Cycle

9. Knowing who our customers are, how they use our services, and how they perceive our services, is an example of which of the Guiding Principles: I) Focus on Value, II) Start where you

are, III) Progress iteratively with feedback, IV) Optimize and automate

A. IV

B. III

C. I

D. II

10. Which one of the following statements is the primary goal of the Service Continuity Management Practice? I) To design and develop the processes and services that continue to operate II) To design the services so that they can resume operations as soon as possible III) To ensure that the services never fail IV) To restore normalcy of the service delivery within agreed business timescales

A. IV

B. II

C. I

D. III

11. Jones, Inc, a large mail order company, is determining what sort of improvements it needs to make to its CRM platform to better support its sales staff and its customers. How will raw technical, process, performance, and value metrics be converted into supporting evidence to help decision makers with their planning?

A. RACI

B. DIKW

C. MTBF

D. PCDA

12. Service improvement opportunities can be documented in a prioritized repository called the…

A. SKMS

B. Continual improvement register (CIR)

C. CMS

D. CMDB

13. Which of the following are the Key Processes as defined by the Continual Improvement Practice for effective implementation of Continual Improvement? I) Service Interface II) 7-Step Improvement Process III) Service Measurement IV) Service Reporting

A. I, II and III

B. I, III and IV

C. III and IV

D. All of these items are key processes of CSI

14. Which of the following items best reflects a decision-making, support, and planning instrument that prepares for the likely consequences of a business action?

   A. Simulation

   B. Analytic model

   C. Return on investment (ROI)

   D. Business case

15. Which implementation approach usually results in an unsuccessful program?

   A. The 4 P's

   B. Big Bang

   C. Timeslicing

   D. Kotter Method

16. Continuous Improvement is all about looking for ways to do which of the following?

   A. Improve service effectiveness

   B. Improve practice efficiency

   C. Improve employee training

   D. Improve cost effectiveness

17. Carpenter Consulting has been experiencing a spike in the level of support calls received over the past week. Many of the incidents reported require immediate attention to minimize disruptions to service. How should the priority of incidents be addressed?

   A. Incidents should be prioritized based on the order each request was received.

   B. Incidents should be prioritized based on their impact and urgency.

   C. Incidents should be prioritized based on the importance/seniority of the person making the request.

   D. Incidents should be prioritized based on the number of people affected for a given disruption.

18. What type of Change follows a pre-existing procedure or work instruction, and does not require an RFC?

   A. Standard

   B. Emergency

   C. Normal

   D. Minor

19. What are the two primary areas of service improvement to be expected from Service Automation? a. Utility b. Warranty c. Security d. Capacity

  A. C and D

  B. B and C

  C. A and D

  D. A and B

20. Markpoint Systems is evaluating its server components in an effort to ensure its infrastructure is suitable for the availability levels it offers its clients. Which of the following uptime measurement would be applied to the hard drive of a server?

  A. Mean Time Between Failures

  B. Mean Time Between System Incidents

  C. Mean Time to Failure

  D. Mean Time to Restore Service

21. Security failures are caused by which of the following? I) Technical errors II) Human errors III) Procedural errors IV) Database failures

  A. II, III and IV

  B. I, III and IV

  C. I, II and III

  D. I, II and IV

22. What type of asset is controlled by Service Configuration Management?

  A. Configuration Item

  B. Service Level Agreement

  C. Software only

  D. Hardware only

23. A team of DBAs is troubleshooting an outage on the main finance database. The outage was reported by a branch office that was unable to access the latest billing information. The investigation of the underlying cause of the outage is known by what term?

  A. Incident Management

  B. Problem Management

  C. Outage Management

  D. Incident Reporting

24. The addition, modification or removal of a CI or Service is performed by _____ _____ _____.

  A. Service Request Management

  B. Change Control Practices

C. Organizational Change Management

D. Service Configuration Management

25. When planning Availability of services, consideration must be given to two areas of Service Management. Those acronyms are ___ and ___.

   A. SVS

   B. VBF and BIA

   C. PIR

   D. BRM

26. No change should be approved without:

   A. Knowing who can legally authorize the change.

   B. Consulting senior management

   C. A backout plan

   D. Reviewing the corporate disaster recovery plan

27. Which of the following is NOT an activity of the Service Level Management Practice? I) Design of appropriate services, technology, practices, information and process measurements to meet the business requirements II) Produce Service Reports and maintain documents related to SLM standards. III) Develop and maintain relationships with all concerned stakeholders of service provision. IV) Record and manage all complaints and compliments.

   A. I only

   B. I and III

   C. II and IV

   D. II only

28. Which of the following is a technical management metric?

   A. Budget variance

   B. Average time to ticket resolution

   C. Pending RFCs

   D. Mean time between failures (MTBF)

29. Knowledge Management is often visualized through what structure?

   A. DIKW- Data, Information, Knowledge, Wisdom

   B. Knowledge Management Database

   C. RACI-Responsible, Accountable, Consulted, Informed

D. Configuration Management Database

30. Identification of critical business processes, potential damage or loss from disruption, resources required to continue critical business processes, maximum permissible total downtime, and maximum permissible time till complete recovery are steps in which Service Continuity Management activity?

   A. Business Impact Analysis
   B. Risk Assessment
   C. Business Continuity and Disaster Recovery
   D. Risk Reduction

31. According to ITIL, proper assessment of a change will provide the answer to how many questions?

   A. 5
   B. 6
   C. 10
   D. Seven

32. Which of the following tasks will a good Service Desk provide? a. Acting as the main source of information to users   b. Identifying the root cause of incidents and creating a workaround   c. To escalate incidents if they cannot be resolved within a specific amount of time   d. Informing users about current or expected errors

   A. A, C, D
   B. B, C, D
   C. A, B, C
   D. All of these responses / All of the above

33. Marco's Car Rental is offering a holiday special of a free day with any rental of 3 days or more. This is an example of performing a _____ _____.

   A. Customer Analysis
   B. Risk analysis
   C. Business Analysis
   D. Evaluation

34. Which of the following groups at Starlight, Inc. is responsible for negotiating SLAs?

   A. Supplier Management
   B. Service Desk
   C. Availability Management
   D. Service Level Management

35. The failure of a Configuration Item (CI), which has not yet impacted service, is known as what?

   A. Alert

   B. Event

   C. Incident

   D. Problem

36. Fill in the blanks: _____ represents all active and inactive services, while _____ consists only of services available at the retail level.

   A. Service Package, Line of Service

   B. Service Catalog, Service Portfolio

   C. The Portfolio, the Service Catalog

   D. Line of Service, Service Package

37. What type of SLA would contain "Corporate level", "Customer level", and "Service level" sub types?

   A. Multi-level Based SLA

   B. Service based SLA

   C. Customer Based SLA

   D. Supplier-based SLA

38. The attributes of a service that have a positive effect on activity performance and represent fitness for purpose, is best reflected by what term?

   A. Value

   B. Utility

   C. Warranty

   D. Service

39. Continual Improvement metrics fall into which three categories?

   A. KPIs, Activity Metrics, Component Metrics

   B. Technology Metrics, Process Metrics, Service Metrics

   C. Performance Metrics, Process Metrics, Service Metrics

   D. Infrastructure Metrics, Process Metrics, Resource Metrics

40. What term best reflects where an organization would store information on the status of all services, including services being developed, services currently offered, and services which have been retired?

   A. Portfolio Management

   B. Service Specification

ITIL Foundation Mock Exam (LITE) 15 - Practice Questions

C. Service Catalogue Management

D. Service Pipeline

ITIL Foundation
Mock Exam (LITE) - 15
Answer Key and Explanations

1. C - As the name suggests, Availability Management ensures agreed levels of availability defined in the SLA is met, and maintains an Availability Plan which reflects the current and future needs of the organization. (Service Management Practices) [Service Management Practices]

2. D - The definition of a Problem is: the unknown root cause of an Incident or series of Incidents. (ITIL Concepts) [ITIL Concepts]

3. D - A baseline must first be established in order to chart performance for future measurements. (Generic Concepts and Definitions) [Generic Concepts and Definitions]

4. D - Configuration Audits verify that CI's exist, and they are correctly recorded. It is appropriate to conduct an audit anytime there is a change in the item's operating environment, when dictated by corporate policy, or when unauthorized CI's are discovered. (ITIL Concepts) [ITIL Concepts]

5. B - Service Level Management requires constant monitoring, reporting, evaluating, and improving of services. Through this ongoing effort, the Service Level Manager identifies and manages improvements to services and processes. (Service Management Practices) [Service Management Practices]

6. C - The objective of the Service Catalog Management Practice is to manage information within the Service Catalog and to ensure accuracy and quality prior to execution into the LIVE environment. (Service Management Practices) [Service Management Practices]

7. C - Notional charging is an approach to charging for IT services, where charges are calculated and customers are informed of the charge, but no money is actually transferred. (Generic Concepts and Definitions) [Generic Concepts and Definitions]

8. A - Workflows and/or process engines allow processes to be pre-defined and controlled, resulting in automatic management of the items described. (ITIL Concepts) [ITIL Concepts]

9. C - Knowing who our customers are, how they use our services, and how they perceive our services, is an example of a Focus on Value. (ITIL Concepts) [ITIL Concepts]

10. A - The primary goal of Service Continuity Management is to restore normalcy of IT service delivery within agreed business timescales. (General Management Practices) [General Management Practices]

11. B - DIKW is an acronym for Data, Information, Knowledge, and

Wisdom. Metrics supply quantitative data. Continual Improvement Practices transforms this data into qualitative information. Combining Information with experience, context, and interpretation, it becomes knowledge. Using DIKW, the leadership team can determine what enhancements should be implemented to meet the needs of internal and external customers. (Generic Concepts and Definitions) [Generic Concepts and Definitions]

12. B - Service improvement opportunities can be documented in a prioritized repository called the Continual improvement register (CIR). (General Management Practices) [General Management Practices]

13. C - Service Measurement and Service Reporting are key practices as defined by the Continual Improvement Practice for effective implementation of Continual Improvement. (General Management Practices) [General Management Practices]

14. D - This statement best describes a Business Case, often used to justify investments in service management. (Service Management Practices) [Service Management Practices]

15. B - A big bang approach does not usually result in a successful improvement program. Step by step approaches such as Deming's PCDA are more successful. (Generic Concepts and Definitions) [Generic Concepts and Definitions]

16. A - Continuous Improvement is all about looking for ways Improve service effectiveness, efficiency and cost effectiveness. (General Management Practices) [General Management Practices]

17. B - When several incidents are being dealt with at the same time, priority must be determined based on the impact and urgency of each incident. (ITIL Concept) [ITIL Concepts]

18. A - A Standard Change is a pre-approved change that is low risk, relatively common, and follows a specific procedure or work instruction. These types of Changes include password resets or providing a replacement keyboard. (Service Management Practices) [Service Management Practices]

19. D - Utility and Warranty are expected to be improved as a result of service automation. (ITIL Concepts) [ITIL Concepts]

20. A - Mean Time Between Failures is a measure of reliability for repairable products. (ITIL Concepts) [ITIL Concepts]

21. C - Security failures are caused by Technical errors, Human errors and Procedural errors. (General Management Practices) [General Management Practices]

22. A - A configuration item is an asset, service component, or other item that

is (or will be) controlled by Service Configuration Management. (Service Management Practices) [Service Management Practices]

23. B - Problem Management involves analyzing and resolving the causes of incidents. (Service Management Practices) [Service Management Practices]

24. B - Change Control Practices manages the addition, modification or removal of a CI or Service. (Service Management Practices) [Service Management Practices]

25. B - Availability must consider Vital Business Functions (VBF) and Business Impact Analysis (BIA) of the internal business customer. (Generic Concepts and Definitions) [Generic Concepts and Definitions]

26. C - No change should be approved without having an answer to the following question: "What will we do if the change is unsuccessful?" You must always ensure that a fallback situation (remediation plan) is available. (Service Management Practices) [Service Management Practices]

27. A - The following are the correct activities of SLM practices: I) Produce Service Reports and maintain documents related to SLM practices. II) Develop and maintain relationships with all concerned stakeholders of service provision. III) Record and manage all complaints and compliments. (Service Management Practices) [Service Management Practices]

28. D - Meantime between failure is a measurement of the interval between failures of a given system component, usually hardware. (ITIL Concepts) [ITIL Concepts]

29. A - The objectives of Knowledge Management include supporting the service provider in order to improve efficiency and quality of services and ensuring that the service provider's staff have adequate information available. Knowledge Management is often visualized as Data, Information, Knowledge, and Wisdom. (General Management Practices) [General Management Practices]

30. A - Business Impact Analysis is concerned with the identification of critical business functions, the consequences of the loss of those functions, and the recovery requirements for those functions. (Generic Concepts and Definitions) [Generic Concepts and Definitions]

31. D - There are seven essential questions that must be answered for a change to be appropriately assessed. These are also known as the 7Rs: Who raised the change? What is the reason for the change? What is the return required from the change? What are the risks involved in the change? What resources are required to deliver the change? Who is responsible for the build, test, and implementation of the

change? What is the relationship between this change and other changes? (ITIL Concepts) [ITIL Concepts]

32. A - Of the items listed, identifying the root cause and creating a workaround is not the role of the Service Desk. (Service Management Practices) [Service Management Practices]

33. C - Performing a business analysis to identify an opportunity for financial gain is part of performing a Business Analysis. (Service Management Practices) [Service Management Practices]

34. D - Negotiating and agreeing upon service levels and documenting SLAs and is the responsibility of Service Level Management. (Service Management Practices) [Service Management Practices]

35. C - Even if the service has not yet been impacted, the failure of a CI is considered an Incident. (Service Management Practices) [Service Management Practices]

36. C - The Portfolio represents all active and inactive services; the Service Catalog contains only active and approved services at a retail level. (Service Management Practices) [Service Management Practices]

37. A - A Multi-level based SLA has three levels of service: Corporate, Customer and Service levels. (Service Management Practices) [Service Management Practices]

38. B - Fitness for purpose describes the concept of "Utility". (ITIL Concepts) [ITIL Concepts]

39. B - The goal of Measurement and Reporting is coordinating the design of metrics, data collection, and reporting activities from other processes. The three types of metrics an organization will need to collect to support Continual Improvement Management as well as other activities are: technology metrics, process metrics, and service metrics. (General Management Practices) [General Management Practices]

40. A - The Portfolio consists of information on the state of services in development (pipeline), services currently being offered (live), and services which have been retired. (General Management Practices) [General Management Practices]

ITIL Foundation Mock Exam (LITE) - 16

Test Name: ITIL Foundation Mock Exam (LITE) - 16
Total Questions: 40
Correct Answers Needed to Pass: 30 (75.00%)
Time Allowed: 60 Minutes

Test Description

This is a cumulative ITIL Foundation test which can be used as a baseline for initial performance. This practice test includes questions from all ITIL question categories.

Test Questions

1. Which of the following methods will assist Logistics, Ltd in identifying places to cut costs while maintaining service quality across the enterprise?

   A. Service provisioning

   B. Decision making framework

   C. Value contribution

   D. Portfolio Management

2. Which of the following items would not be a Key Performance Indicator (KPI) of Service Catalogue Management?

   A. The percentage of services which have been delivered, in relation to the total amount of services which exist in the Service Catalogue

   B. Number of incidents handled by the Service Desk using information stored in the Service Catalogue

   C. The amount of differences discovered between information stored in the Service Catalogue, and the actual state of services maintained by the organization

   D. The percentage of Service Level Agreement infractions incurred by the performing organization

3. How is service value calculated?

   A. Service Utility + Service Cost

   B. Service Uptime + Service Utilization

   C. Service Cost + Service Features

   D. Utility + Warranty

4. Which of the following are NOT activities related to the Strategy Management Practice? I) Survey the market and understand the needs of the market. II) Articulate the needs of the customer and define the value of your service in those terms. III) Analyze the business patterns and prescribe the way in which they will access the service over a period of time. IV) Agreeing upon Service Level Targets with the customer after negotiation to produce the SLA.

   A. I and II

   B. I and III

   C. Only II

   D. III and IV

5. Deploying a new web browser to all users in the finance department as part of a quarterly update package is an example of what type of change?

   A. Technology change

   B. Regular change

   C. Standard change

   D. Version change

6. When applied properly, which of the following items are expected to be reduced by service automation? a. Costs b. Quality c. Warranty d. Risks

   A. A and D

   B. A and B

   C. B and C

   D. C and D

7. Service Level Agreement negotiation occurs in which Category of ITIL Practices?

   A. Service Operation

   B. Service Transition

   C. Continual Improvement

   D. Service Management Practices

8. What are the contents of a Service Catalog?

   A. A Service Catalog contains a list of decommissioned services provided by the Service Provider.

ITIL Foundation Mock Exam (LITE) 16 - Practice Questions

B. A Service Catalog contains a list of retired services provided by the Service Provider.

C. A Service Catalog contains a list of live, retired and decommissioned services provided by the Service Provider.

D. A Service Catalog contains a list of live services provided by the Service Provider.

9. The Finance Department at ACME Widgets is asking the IT team for the business justification to purchase and implement a CMDB system. Currently they do not have a unified CMDB. Data is stored on several different systems and maintained by different groups. Which of the following would be appropriate justifications?

A. Data is available to all staff

B. One single system to support.

C. Possible cost savings related to identifying duplicate services.

D. All of the above

10. Services provide _____ created by one or more of its resources and capabilities.

A. Warranty

B. Value

C. Improvements

D. Security

11. Which of the following define how Change Control will be managed, including roles, responsibilities, and escalation processes?

A. Change control

B. Change model

C. Configuration management

D. Change log

12. Which of the following are used to judge the effectiveness and efficiency of SLM activities? I) KPI II) Metrics III) SIP

A. I and III only

B. I, II and III

C. None of these items are used to judge the effectiveness and efficiency of SLM activities

D. I and II only

13. ABC Plastics has decided to move its IT services from a 3rd party vendor to a shared services group within its parent company. What is this type of change called?

    A. Insourcing

    B. Aggregation

    C. Corporate reorganization

    D. Functional reorganization

14. Fill in the blank: A _____ is the addition, modification, or elimination of an authorized, planned, or supporting service and its related documentation.

    A. Service asset and configuration management

    B. Continual Service Improvement

    C. Change

    D. Baseline review

15. Melissa is documenting availability metrics for her management team. She includes a term that refers to the uptime of a service and calculated as the average time between the recovery of one incident and the occurrence of the next. What is this term?

    A. MTRS

    B. MTBSI

    C. MTBR

    D. MTBF

16. Michael is responsible for specific services at his company. He attends Change Advisory Board meetings when they are relevant to his services, he maintains the service description in the Service Catalog, and he measures the performance and availability of the service. What is Michael's role called?

    A. Service Catalog Manager

    B. Process Owner

    C. IT Manager

    D. Service Owner

ITIL Foundation Mock Exam (LITE) 16 - Practice Questions

17. To ensure a shared understanding of the vision, current status, and improvement direction of the organization is the purpose of the which Value Chain Activity?

A. Plan

B. Obtain/Build

C. Improve

D. Deliver and Support

18. What type of study should be done to determine the ramifications of a specific Event at an organization?

A. PDCA

B. Gap Analysis

C. Return on Investment

D. Business Impact Analysis

19. What does the acronym RACI stand for?

A. Risks, Actions, Completion, Investigation

B. References, Acceptance, Control, Integration

C. Requirements, Availability, Computers, Information

D. Responsible, Accountable, Consulted, Informed

20. The RACI model is a useful tool which helps in which of the following activities?

A. RACI model is used in only measuring the effectiveness of processes.

B. RACI model is used in designing activities and functions.

C. RACI model is used to assign roles in a project or other activity.

D. RACI model is used in designing an organization's policies.

21. The significance of the RACI model is BEST described in which of the following statements?

A. Each activity in a process should be assigned a role: Responsible, Accountable, Consulted or Informed and only one person can be Accountable.

B. Each activity in a process should have at least one person as

Accountable and only one person as Responsible.

C. Each activity in a process should have one person as Responsible owner and any number of persons as Accountable.

D. Each activity in a process should have only one person as Responsible owner and only one person as Accountable.

22. Marissa has just joined the IT department at a large chain of department stores as part of the design team. Her manager has provided her with a binder that contains all the information needed to provide guidance and structure for the life of a specific service. A new version of this documentation is produced for every new service, major changes to a service, or the retirement of a service. What is this information package called?

A. Service Design Package

B. Service Index

C. Service Catalog

D. Service Portfolio

23. Which of the following would not be a likely key metric for the Incident Management Practice?

A. Total number of incidents logged in the past month

B. Total number of major incidents

C. Average cost to resolve each incident

D. Time to resolve underlying root cause and prevent recurring incidents

24. Of the items below, what information would the Service Desk provide to the IT management of an organization?

A. The number of successfully implemented changes

B. The number of resolved problems, and the reduction in related incidents

C. The number of calls handled by the Service Desk overall, and by workstation

D. The cost of implemented changes

25. Establishing remediation plans in the event of a deployment failure, and

ITIL Foundation Mock Exam (LITE) 16 - Practice Questions

creating test plans, happen during which ITIL Practice?

A. Change Control

B. Deployment Management

C. Release Management

D. Service Design

26. In which ITIL Practice would the Denali Integration Partners strategy team ask the question "have we reached our improvement goals?"

A. Service Definition

B. Service Strategy

C. Service Support

D. Continual Improvement

27. "A set of specialized organizational capabilities for enabling value for customers in the form of services" is ITIL's definition of _____ _____.

A. Client Services

B. Internal Support

C. Customer Service

D. Service Management

28. Which of the following would NOT be an attribute of a CI?

A. Value after depreciation

B. Installation instructions

C. Purchase price

D. Comments

29. Which of the items below represents a service provider's investments across all market spaces, and includes the Service Catalogue, Service Pipeline, and Retired Services?

A. Customer Assets

B. Service Portfolio

C. Market Space

D. Service Lifecycle

30. The "R-A-C-I" in the RACI model stand for which one of the following?

A. RACI stands for Reform-Accountability-Consult-Inform.

B. RACI stands for Responsible-Accountable-Consulted-Informed.

C. RACI stands for Responsibility-Accountability-Consult-Information.

D. RACI stands for Responsibility-Accounts-Consult-Inform.

ITIL Foundation
Mock Exam (LITE) - 16
Answer Key and Explanations

1. **D** - Portfolio Management is a dynamic method to govern investments in Service Management across the enterprise in terms of financial values. (General Management Practices) [General Management Practices]

2. **D** - The percentage of Service Level Agreement infractions incurred by the performing organization pertains to Service Level Management, not Service Catalogue Management. (Service Management Practices) [Service Management Practices]

3. **D** - Service value is the sum of Utility (fitness of purpose, or what the service does) and Warranty (fitness of use, or how well the service performs). (ITIL Concepts) [ITIL Concepts]

4. **D** - The Strategy Management Practice is concerned with strategizing the conception of the service as per the market demand, development of the service, planning for the resources and execution. The following are some of the key activities: Survey the market and understand the needs of the market; Identify your customers and zero in on them; Articulate the needs of the customer and define the value for your service in those terms; Define the kinds of services as a service provider you can provide to the customer; To define the value add you can provide to your customers. (General Management Practices) [General Management Practices]

5. **C** - A Standard Change is a change of a service or infrastructure component that Change Control must register, but is of low risk and is pre-authorized. These are routine changes, such as PC upgrades. (Service Management Practices) [Service Management Practices]

6. **A** - When applied properly, costs and risks are expected to be reduced by service automation. (Generic Concepts and Practices) [Generic Concepts and Definitions]

7. **D** - Within Service Management Practices, Service Level Management is concerned with negotiating and agreeing upon SLAs. (Service Management Practices) [Service Management Practices]

8. **D** - A service Catalog contains a list of live services provided by the Service Provider. (Service Management Practices) [Service Management Practices]

9. D - The benefits of a CMDB include reduction in support costs by using a single system rather than multiple, disparate tools and increased visibility into service offerings, consistency in CI data and access to CI data. (Service Management Practices) [Service Management Practices]

10. B - Services provide Value created by one or more of its resources and capabilities. (ITIL Concepts) [ITIL Concepts]

11. B - A Change Model defines how changes are to be handled. Each organization must define its own Change Model; there may be multiple Change Models in place in a single organization to support a variety of change types. (ITIL Concepts) [ITIL Concepts]

12. B - Key Performance Indicators (KPIs), Metrics and Service Improvement Plans (SIPs) are used to judge the effectiveness and efficiency of SLM activities. (ITIL Concepts) [ITIL Concepts]

13. A - Migration from a Type III to a Type II service provider is called insourcing. (Service Management Practices) [Service Management Practices]

14. C - A Change is the addition, modification, or elimination of an authorized, planned, or supporting service and its related documentation. (Service Management Practices) [Service Management Practices]

15. D - MTBF, Mean Time Between Failures, is a measure of uptime, and is an indicator of the reliability of the service. (ITIL Concepts) [ITIL Concepts]

16. D - The Service Owner is the primary point of contact for a specific service, and owns and represents that service for the organization. (Service Management Practices) [Service Management Practices]

17. A - To ensure a shared understanding of the vision, current status, and improvement direction of the organization is the purpose of the "Plan" Value Chain Activity? (SVC) [SVC - Service Value Chain]

18. D - A Business Impact Analysis (BIA) studies a specific Event, such as a power outage or flood, and the possible results the Event could have on a company. (Generic Concepts and Definitions) [Generic Concepts and Definitions]

19. D - RACI is an acronym for the four most important roles to be defined in

a service. Each letter stands for an answer to the questions: "Who is?" Responsible, Accountable, Consulted, and Informed." (Generic Concepts and Definitions) [Generic Concepts and Definitions]

20. C - RACI model is used in assigning roles and responsibilities of activity. (Generic Concepts and Definitions) [Generic Concepts and Definitions]

21. A - Each activity in a process should have at least one person as Responsible and only one person as Accountable for the activity. (Generic Concepts and Definitions) [Generic Concepts and Definitions]

22. A - The information contained within a Service Design Package includes all aspects of the service and its requirements, and is used to provide guidance through all the subsequent stages of its lifecycle. It contains information such as requirements, user acceptance criteria, and service transition plans. (Service Management Practices) [Service Management Practices]

23. D - Problem Management would be responsible for the time to resolve underlying root cause and prevent recurring incidents, not Incident Management. (Service Management Practices) [Service Management Practices]

24. C - Of the options listed, the Service Desk would report on the number of calls handled in total and by workstation. Resolved problems relate to Problem Management, and changes relate to Change Control. (Service Management Practices) [Service Management Practices]

25. A - Change Control is responsible for the planning of fail situations and the test plans that are needed to ensure a service is running appropriately before it is deployed. (Service Management Practices) [Service Management Practices]

26. D - As part of Continual Improvement, an organization may conduct an implementation review to determine whether improvements have produced the desired effects. (Service Management Practices) [Service Management Practices]

27. D - Service Management is defined as: "A set of specialized organizational capabilities for enabling value for customers in the form of services" is ITIL's definition of Service Management. (Service Management Practices) [Service Management Practices]

28. B - Attributes are identifying information about a CI. Installation instructions would not be an attribute, but rather would be controlled as a CI. (ITIL Concepts) [ITIL Concepts]

29. B - The Service Portfolio encompasses the Service Catalogue, Service Pipeline, and Retired Services. (ITIL Concepts) [ITIL Concepts]

30. B - RACI stands for Responsible-Accountable-Consulted-Informed. (Generic Concepts and Definitions) [Generic Concepts and Definitions]

ITIL 4 Glossary and Key Terms

Copyright © AXELOS Limited 2019. All rights reserved. Material is reproduced with the permission of AXELOS

acceptance criteria	A list of minimum requirements that a service or service component must meet for it to be acceptable to key stakeholders.
Agile	An umbrella term for a collection of frameworks and techniques that together enable teams and individuals to work in a way that is typified by collaboration, prioritization, iterative and incremental delivery, and timeboxing. There are several specific methods (or frameworks) that are classed as Agile, such as Scrum, Lean, and Kanban.
architecture management practice	The practice of providing an understanding of all the different elements that make up an organization and how those elements relate to one another.
asset register	A database or list of assets, capturing key attributes such as ownership and financial value.
availability	The ability of an IT service or other configuration item to perform its agreed function when required.
availability management practice	The practice of ensuring that services deliver agreed levels of availability to meet the needs of customers and users.
baseline	A report or metric that serves as a starting point against which progress or change can be assessed.
best practice	A way of working that has been proven to be successful by multiple organizations.
big data	The use of very large volumes of structured and unstructured data from a variety of sources to gain new insights.

business analysis practice	The practice of analyzing a business or some element of a business, defining its needs and recommending solutions to address these needs and/or solve a business problem, and create value for stakeholders.
business case	A justification for expenditure of organizational resources, providing information about costs, benefits, options, risks, and issues.
business impact analysis (BIA)	A key activity in the practice of service continuity management that identifies vital business functions and their dependencies.
business relationship manager (BRM)	A role responsible for maintaining good relationships with one or more customers.
call	An interaction (e.g. a telephone call) with the service desk. A call could result in an incident or a service request being logged.
call/contact center	An organization or business unit that handles large numbers of incoming and outgoing calls and other interactions.
capability	The ability of an organization, person, process, application, configuration item, or IT service to carry out an activity.
capacity and performance management practice	The practice of ensuring that services achieve agreed and expected performance levels, satisfying current and future demand in a cost-effective way.
capacity planning	The activity of creating a plan that manages resources to meet demand for services.
change	The addition, modification, or removal of anything that could have a direct or indirect effect on services.
change authority	A person or group responsible for authorizing a change.

change control practice	The practice of ensuring that risks are properly assessed, authorizing changes to proceed and managing a change schedule in order to maximize the number of successful service and product changes.
change model	A repeatable approach to the management of a particular type of change.
change schedule	A calendar that shows planned and historical changes.
charging	The activity that assigns a price for services.
cloud computing	A model for enabling on-demand network access to a shared pool of configurable computing resources that can be rapidly provided with minimal management effort or provider interaction.
compliance	The act of ensuring that a standard or set of guidelines is followed, or that proper, consistent accounting or other practices are being employed.
confidentiality	A security objective that ensures information is not made available or disclosed to unauthorized entities.
configuration	An arrangement of configuration items (CIs) or other resources that work together to deliver a product or service. Can also be used to describe the parameter settings for one or more CIs.
configuration item (CI)	Any component that needs to be managed in order to deliver an IT service.
configuration management database (CMDB)	A database used to store configuration records throughout their lifecycle. The CMDB also maintains the relationships between configuration records.

configuration management system (CMS)	A set of tools, data, and information that is used to support service configuration management.
configuration record	A record containing the details of a configuration item (CI). Each configuration record documents the lifecycle of a single CI. Configuration records are stored in a configuration management database.
continual improvement practice	The practice of aligning an organization's practices and services with changing business needs through the ongoing identification and improvement of all elements involved in the effective management of products and services.
continuous deployment	An integrated set of practices and tools used to deploy software changes into the production environment. These software changes have already passed pre-defined automated tests.
continuous integration / continuous delivery	An integrated set of practices and tools used to merge developers' code, build and test the resulting software, and package it so that it is ready for deployment.
control	The means of managing a risk, ensuring that a business objective is achieved, or that a process is followed.
cost	The amount of money spent on a specific activity or resource.
cost center	A business unit or project to which costs are assigned.
critical success factor (CSF)	A necessary precondition for the achievement of intended results.
culture	A set of values that is shared by a group of people, including expectations about how people should behave, ideas, beliefs, and practices.

ITIL Glossary

customer	A person who defines the requirements for a service and takes responsibility for the outcomes of service consumption.
customer experience (CX)	The sum of functional and emotional interactions with a service and service provider as perceived by a service consumer.
dashboard	A real-time graphical representation of data.
deliver and support	The value chain activity that ensures services are delivered and supported according to agreed specifications and stakeholders' expectations.
demand	Input to the service value system based on opportunities and needs from internal and external stakeholders.
deployment	The movement of any service component into any environment.
deployment management practice	The practice of moving new or changed hardware, software, documentation, processes, or any other service component to live environments.
design and transition	The value chain activity that ensures products and services continually meet stakeholder expectations for quality, costs, and time to market.
design thinking	A practical and human-centered approach used by product and service designers to solve complex problems and find practical and creative solutions that meet the needs of an organization and its customers.
development environment	An environment used to create or modify IT services or applications.
DevOps	An organizational culture that aims to improve the flow of value to customers. DevOps focuses on culture, automation, Lean, measurement, and sharing (CALMS).

digital transformation	The evolution of traditional business models to meet the needs of highly empowered customers, with technology playing an enabling role.
disaster	A sudden unplanned event that causes great damage or serious loss to an organization. A disaster results in an organization failing to provide critical business functions for some predetermined minimum period of time.
disaster recovery plans	A set of clearly defined plans related to how an organization will recover from a disaster as well as return to a pre-disaster condition, considering the four dimensions of service management.
driver	Something that influences strategy, objectives, or requirements.
effectiveness	A measure of whether the objectives of a practice, service or activity have been achieved.
efficiency	A measure of whether the right amount of resources have been used by a practice, service, or activity.
emergency change	A change that must be introduced as soon as possible.
engage	The value chain activity that provides a good understanding of stakeholder needs, transparency, continual engagement, and good relationships with all stakeholders.
environment	A subset of the IT infrastructure that is used for a particular purpose, for example a live environment or test environment. Can also mean the external conditions that influence or affect something.
error	A flaw or vulnerability that may cause incidents.
error control	Problem management activities used to manage known errors.

ITIL Glossary

escalation	The act of sharing awareness or transferring ownership of an issue or work item.
event	Any change of state that has significance for the management of a service or other configuration item.
external customer	A customer who works for an organization other than the service provider.
failure	A loss of ability to operate to specification, or to deliver the required output or outcome.
feedback loop	A technique whereby the outputs of one part of a system are used as inputs to the same part of the system.
four dimensions of service management	The four perspectives that are critical to the effective and efficient facilitation of value for customers and other stakeholders in the form of products and services.
goods	Tangible resources that are transferred or available for transfer from a service provider to a service consumer, together with ownership and associated rights and responsibilities.
governance	The means by which an organization is directed and controlled.
identity	A unique name that is used to identify and grant system access rights to a user, person, or role.
improve	The value chain activity that ensures continual improvement of products, services, and practices across all value chain activities and the four dimensions of service management.
incident	An unplanned interruption to a service or reduction in the quality of a service.

ITIL Glossary

incident management	The practice of minimizing the negative impact of incidents by restoring normal service operation as quickly as possible.
information and technology	One of the four dimensions of service management. It includes the information and knowledge used to deliver services, and the information and technologies used to manage all aspects of the service value system.
information security management practice	The practice of protecting an organization by understanding and managing risks to the confidentiality, integrity, and availability of information.
information security policy	The policy that governs an organization's approach to information security management.
infrastructure and platform management practice	The practice of overseeing the infrastructure and platforms used by an organization. This enables the monitoring of technology solutions available, including solutions from third parties.
integrity	A security objective that ensures information is only modified by authorized personnel and activities.
internal customer	A customer who works for the same organization as the service provider.
Internet of Things	The interconnection of devices via the internet that were not traditionally thought of as IT assets, but now include embedded computing capability and network connectivity.
IT asset	Any financially valuable component that can contribute to the delivery of an IT product or service.
IT asset management practice	The practice of planning and managing the full lifecycle of all IT assets.
IT infrastructure	All of the hardware, software, networks, and facilities that are required to develop, test, deliver, monitor, manage, and support IT services.

IT service	A service based on the use of information technology.
ITIL	Best-practice guidance for IT service management.
ITIL guiding principles	Recommendations that can guide an organization in all circumstances, regardless of changes in its goals, strategies, type of work, or management structure.
ITIL service value chain	An operating model for service providers that covers all the key activities required to effectively manage products and services.
Kanban	A method for visualizing work, identifying potential blockages and resource conflicts, and managing work in progress.
key performance indicator (KPI)	An important metric used to evaluate the success in meeting an objective.
knowledge management practice	The practice of maintaining and improving the effective, efficient, and convenient use of information and knowledge across an organization.
known error	A problem that has been analyzed but has not been resolved.
Lean	An approach that focuses on improving workflows by maximizing value through the elimination of waste.
lifecycle	The full set of stages, transitions, and associated statuses in the life of a service, product, practice, or other entity.
live	Refers to a service or other configuration item operating in the live environment.
live environment	A controlled environment used in the delivery of IT services to service consumers.
maintainability	The ease with which a service or other entity can be repaired or modified.
major incident	An incident with significant business impact, requiring an immediate coordinated resolution.

management system	Interrelated or interacting elements that establish policy and objectives and enable the achievement of those objectives.
maturity	A measure of the reliability, efficiency and effectiveness of an organization, practice, or process.
mean time between failures (MTBF)	A metric of how frequently a service or other configuration item fails.
mean time to restore service (MTRS)	A metric of how quickly a service is restored after a failure.
measurement and reporting	The practice of supporting good decision-making and continual improvement by decreasing levels of uncertainty.
metric	A measurement or calculation that is monitored or reported for management and improvement.
minimum viable product (MVP)	A product with just enough features to satisfy early customers, and to provide feedback for future product development.
mission statement	A short but complete description of the overall purpose and intentions of an organization. It states what is to be achieved, but not how this should be done.
model	A representation of a system, practice, process, service, or other entity that is used to understand and predict its behavior and relationships.
modelling	The activity of creating, maintaining, and utilizing models.
monitoring	Repeated observation of a system, practice, process, service, or other entity to detect events and to ensure that the current status is known.
monitoring and event management practice	The practice of systematically observing services and service components, and recording and reporting selected changes of state identified as events.

obtain/build	The value chain activity that ensures service components are available when and where they are needed, and that they meet agreed specifications.
operation	The routine running and management of an activity, product, service, or other configuration item.
operational technology	The hardware and software solutions that detect or cause changes in physical processes through direct monitoring and/or control of physical devices such as valves, pumps, etc.
organization	A person or a group of people that has its own functions with responsibilities, authorities, and relationships to achieve its objectives.
organizational change management practice	The practice of ensuring that changes in an organization are smoothly and successfully implemented and that lasting benefits are achieved by managing the human aspects of the changes.
organizational resilience	The ability of an organization to anticipate, prepare for, respond to, and adapt to unplanned external influences.
organizational velocity	The speed, effectiveness, and efficiency with which an organization operates. Organizational velocity influences time to market, quality, safety, costs, and risks.
organizations and people	One of the four dimensions of service management. It ensures that the way an organization is structured and managed, as well as its roles, responsibilities, and systems of authority and communication, is well defined and supports its overall strategy and operating model.
outcome	A result for a stakeholder enabled by one or more outputs.
output	A tangible or intangible deliverable of an activity.

outsourcing	The process of having external suppliers provide products and services that were previously provided internally.
partners and suppliers	One of the four dimensions of service management. It encompasses the relationships an organization has with other organizations that are involved in the design, development, deployment, delivery, support, and/or continual improvement of services.
partnership	A relationship between two organizations that involves working closely together to achieve common goals and objectives.
performance	A measure of what is achieved or delivered by a system, person, team, practice, or service.
pilot	A test implementation of a service with a limited scope in a live environment.
plan	The value chain activity that ensures a shared understanding of the vision, current status, and improvement direction for all four dimensions and all products and services across an organization.
policy	Formally documented management expectations and intentions, used to direct decisions and activities.
portfolio management practice	The practice of ensuring that an organization has the right mix of programmes, projects, products, and services to execute its strategy within its funding and resource constraints.
post-implementation review (PIR)	A review after the implementation of a change, to evaluate success and identify opportunities for improvement.
practice	A set of organizational resources designed for performing work or accomplishing an objective.

problem	A cause, or potential cause, of one or more incidents.
problem management practice	The practice of reducing the likelihood and impact of incidents by identifying actual and potential causes of incidents, and managing workarounds and known errors.
procedure	A documented way to carry out an activity or a process.
process	A set of interrelated or interacting activities that transform inputs into outputs. A process takes one or more defined inputs and turns them into defined outputs. Processes define the sequence of actions and their dependencies.
product	A configuration of an organization's resources designed to offer value for a consumer.
production environment	See live environment.
programme	A set of related projects and activities, and an organization structure created to direct and oversee them.
project	A temporary structure that is created for the purpose of delivering one or more outputs (or products) according to an agreed business case.
project management practice	The practice of ensuring that all an organization's projects are successfully delivered.
quick win	An improvement that is expected to provide a return on investment in a short period of time with relatively small cost and effort.
record	A document stating results achieved and providing evidence of activities performed.

ITIL Glossary

recovery	The activity of returning a configuration item to normal operation after a failure.
recovery point objective (RPO)	The point to which information used by an activity must be restored to enable the activity to operate on resumption.
recovery time objective (RTO)	The maximum acceptable period of time following a service disruption that can elapse before the lack of business functionality severely impacts the organization.
relationship management practice	The practice of establishing and nurturing links between an organization and its stakeholders at strategic and tactical levels.
release	A version of a service or other configuration item, or a collection of configuration items, that is made available for use.
release management practice	The practice of making new and changed services and features available for use.
reliability	The ability of a product, service, or other configuration item to perform its intended function for a specified period of time or number of cycles.
request catalogue	A view of the service catalogue, providing details on service requests for existing and new services, which is made available for the user.
request for change (RFC)	A description of a proposed change used to initiate change control.
resolution	The action of solving an incident or problem.
resource	A person, or other entity, that is required for the execution of an activity or the achievement of an objective. Resources used by an organization may be owned by the organization or used according to an agreement with the resource owner.

retire	The act of permanently withdrawing a product, service, or other configuration item from use.
risk	A possible event that could cause harm or loss, or make it more difficult to achieve objectives. Can also be defined as uncertainty of outcome, and can be used in the context of measuring the probability of positive outcomes as well as negative outcomes.
risk assessment	An activity to identify, analyze, and evaluate risks.
risk management practice	The practice of ensuring that an organization understands and effectively handles risks.
service	A means of enabling value co-creation by facilitating outcomes that customers want to achieve, without the customer having to manage specific costs and risks.
service action	Any action required to deliver a service output to a user. Service actions may be performed by a service provider resource, by service users, or jointly.
service architecture	A view of all the services provided by an organization. It includes interactions between the services, and service models that describe the structure and dynamics of each service.
service catalogue	Structured information about all the services and service offerings of a service provider, relevant for a specific target audience.
service catalogue management practice	The practice of providing a single source of consistent information on all services and service offerings, and ensuring that it is available to the relevant audience.

service configuration management practice	The practice of ensuring that accurate and reliable information about the configuration of services, and the configuration items that support them, is available when and where needed.
service consumption	Activities performed by an organization to consume services. It includes the management of the consumer's resources needed to use the service, service actions performed by users, and the receiving (acquiring) of goods (if required).
service continuity management practice	The practice of ensuring that service availability and performance are maintained at a sufficient level in case of a disaster.
service design practice	The practice of designing products and services that are fit for purpose, fit for use, and that can be delivered by the organization and its ecosystem.
service desk	The point of communication between the service provider and all its users.
service desk practice	The practice of capturing demand for incident resolution and service requests.
service financial management practice	The practice of supporting an organization's strategies and plans for service management by ensuring that the organization's financial resources and investments are being used effectively.
service level	One or more metrics that define expected or achieved service quality.
service level agreement (SLA)	A documented agreement between a service provider and a customer that identifies both services required and the expected level of service.
service level management practice	The practice of setting clear business-based targets for service performance so that the delivery of a service can be properly assessed, monitored, and managed against these targets.

service management	A set of specialized organizational capabilities for enabling value for customers in the form of services.
service offering	A formal description of one or more services, designed to address the needs of a target consumer group. A service offering may include goods, access to resources, and service actions.
service owner	A role that is accountable for the delivery of a specific service.
service portfolio	A complete set of products and services that are managed throughout their lifecycles by an organization.
service provider	A role performed by an organization in a service relationship to provide services to consumers.
service provision	Activities performed by an organization to provide services. It includes management of the provider's resources, configured to deliver the service; ensuring access to these resources for users; fulfilment of the agreed service actions; service level management; and continual improvement. It may also include the supply of goods.
service relationship	A cooperation between a service provider and service consumer. Service relationships include service provision, service consumption, and service relationship management.
service relationship management	Joint activities performed by a service provider and a service consumer to ensure continual value co-creation based on agreed and available service offerings.
service request	A request from a user or a user's authorized representative that initiates a service action which has been agreed as a normal part of service delivery.

service request management practice	The practice of supporting the agreed quality of a service by handling all pre-defined, user-initiated service requests in an effective and user-friendly manner.
service validation and testing practice	The practice of ensuring that new or changed products and services meet defined requirements.
service value system (SVS)	A model representing how all the components and activities of an organization work together to facilitate value creation.
software development and management practice	The practice of ensuring that applications meet stakeholder needs in terms of functionality, reliability, maintainability, compliance, and auditability.
sourcing	The activity of planning and obtaining resources from a particular source type, which could be internal or external, centralized or distributed, and open or proprietary.
specification	A documented description of the properties of a product, service, or other configuration item.
sponsor	A person who authorizes budget for service consumption. Can also be used to describe an organization or individual that provides financial or other support for an initiative.
stakeholder	A person or organization that has an interest or involvement in an organization, product, service, practice, or other entity.
standard	A document, established by consensus and approved by a recognized body, that provides for common and repeated use, mandatory requirements, guidelines, or characteristics for its subject.
standard change	A low-risk, pre-authorized change that is well understood and fully documented, and which can be implemented without needing additional authorization.

status	A description of the specific states an entity can have at a given time.
strategy management practice	The practice of formulating the goals of an organization and adopting the courses of action and allocation of resources necessary for achieving those goals.
supplier	A stakeholder responsible for providing services that are used by an organization.
supplier management practice	The practice of ensuring that an organization's suppliers and their performance levels are managed appropriately to support the provision of seamless quality products and services.
support team	A team with the responsibility to maintain normal operations, address users' requests, and resolve incidents and problems related to specified products, services, or other configuration items.
system	A combination of interacting elements organized and maintained to achieve one or more stated purposes.
systems thinking	A holistic approach to analysis that focuses on the way that a system's constituent parts work, interrelate, and interact over time, and within the context of other systems.
technical debt	The total rework backlog accumulated by choosing workarounds instead of system solutions that would take longer.
test environment	A controlled environment established to test products, services, and other configuration items.
third party	A stakeholder external to an organization.
throughput	A measure of the amount of work performed by a product, service, or other system over a given period of time.

transaction	A unit of work consisting of an exchange between two or more participants or systems.
use case	A technique using realistic practical scenarios to define functional requirements and to design tests.
user	A person who uses services.
utility	The functionality offered by a product or service to meet a particular need. Utility can be summarized as 'what the service does' and can be used to determine whether a service is 'fit for purpose'. To have utility, a service must either support the performance of the consumer or remove constraints from the consumer. Many services do both.
utility requirements	Functional requirements which have been defined by the customer and are unique to a specific product.
validation	Confirmation that the system, product, service, or other entity meets the agreed specification.
value	The perceived benefits, usefulness, and importance of something.
value stream	A series of steps an organization undertakes to create and deliver products and services to consumers.
value streams and processes	One of the four dimensions of service management. It defines the activities, workflows, controls, and procedures needed to achieve the agreed objectives.

vision	A defined aspiration of what an organization would like to become in the future.
warranty	Assurance that a product or service will meet agreed requirements. Warranty can be summarized as 'how the service performs' and can be used to determine whether a service is 'fit for use'. Warranty often relates to service levels aligned with the needs of service consumers. This may be based on a formal agreement, or it may be a marketing message or brand image. Warranty typically addresses such areas as the availability of the service, its capacity, levels of security, and continuity. A service may be said to provide acceptable assurance, or 'warranty', if all defined and agreed conditions are met.
warranty requirements	Typically non-functional requirements captured as inputs from key stakeholders and other practices.
waterfall method	A development approach that is linear and sequential with distinct objectives for each phase of development.
work instruction	A detailed description to be followed in order to perform an activity.
workaround	A solution that reduces or eliminates the impact of an incident or problem for which a full resolution is not yet available. Some workarounds reduce the likelihood of incidents.
workforce and talent management practice	The practice of ensuring that an organization has the right people with the appropriate skills and knowledge and in the correct roles to support its business objectives.

ITIL Glossary

ITIL Exam Taking Tips

ITIL Glossary

Exam Taking Tips

Studying for a multiple choice exam entails preparing in a unique way as opposed to other types of tests. The ITIL Foundation exam asks one to recognize correct answers among a set of four options. The extra options that are not the correct answer are called the "distracters"; and their purpose, unsurprisingly, is to distract the test taker from the actual correct answer among the bunch.

Students usually consider multiple choice exams as much easier than other types of exams; this is not necessarily true with the ITIL Foundation exam. Among these reasons are:

- Most multiple choice exams ask for simple, factual information; unlike the Foundation exam which often requires the student to apply knowledge and make a best judgment.

- The majority of multiple choice exams involve a large quantity of different questions – so even if you get a few incorrect, it's still okay. The Foundation exam covers a broad set of material, often times in greater depth than other certification exams.

Regardless of whether or not multiple choice testing is more forgiving; in reality, one must study immensely because of the sheer volume of information that is covered.

Although 60 minutes may seem like more than enough time for a multiple choice exam of 40 questions; time management remains a crucial factor in succeeding and doing well. You should always try and answer all of the questions you are confident about first, and then go back to those items you are not sure about afterwards. Always read *carefully* through the entire test as well, and do your best to not leave any question blank upon submission– even if you do not readily know the answer.

Many people do very well with reading through each question and not looking at the options before trying to answer. This way, they can steer clear (usually) of being fooled by one of the "distracter" options or get into a tug-of-war between two choices that both have a good chance of being the actual answer.

Never assume that "all of the above" or "none of the above" answers are the actual choice. Many times they are, but in recent years they have been used much more frequently as distracter options on standardized tests. Typically this is done in an effort to get people to stop believing the myth that they are always the correct answer.

You should be careful of negative answers as well. These answers contain words such as "none", "not", "neither", and the like. Despite often times being very confusing, if you read these types of questions and answers carefully, then you should be able to piece together which is the correct answer. Just take your time!

Never try to overanalyze a question, or try and think about how the test givers are trying to lead astray potential test takers. Keep it simple and stay with what you know.

If you ever narrow down a question to two possible answers, then try and slow down your thinking and think about how the two different options/answers differ. Look at the question again and try to apply how this difference between the two potential answers relates to the question. If you are convinced there is literally no difference between the two potential answers (you'll more than likely be wrong in assuming this), then take another look at the answers that you've already eliminated. Perhaps one of them is actually the correct one and you'd made a previously unforeseen mistake.

On occasion, over-generalizations are used within response options to mislead test takers. To help guard against this, always be wary of responses/answers that use absolute words like "always", or "never". These are less likely to actually be the answer than phrases like "probably" or "usually" are. Funny or witty responses are also, most of the time, incorrect – so steer clear of those as much as possible.

Although you should always take each question individually, "none of the above" answers are usually less likely to be the correct selection than "all of the above" is. Keep this in mind with the understanding that it is not an absolute rule, and should be analyzed on a case-by-case (or "question-by-question") basis.

Looking for grammatical errors can also be a huge clue. If the stem ends with an indefinite article such as "an" then you'll probably do well to look for an answer that begins with a vowel instead of a consonant. Also, the longest response is also oftentimes the correct one, since whoever wrote the question item may have tended to load the answer with qualifying adjectives or phrases in an effort to make it correct. Again though, always deal with these on a question-by-question basis, because you could very easily be getting a question where this does not apply.

Verbal associations are oftentimes critical because a response may repeat a key word that was in the question. Always be on the alert for this. Playing the old Sesame Street game "Which of these things is not like the other" is also a very solid strategy, if a bit preschool. Sometimes many of a question's distracters will be very similar to try to trick you into thinking that one choice is related to the other. The answer very well could be completely unrelated however, so stay alert.

Just because you have finished a practice test, be aware that you are not done working. After you have graded your test with all of the necessary corrections, review it and try to recognize what happened in the answers that you got wrong. Did you simply not know the qualifying correct information? Perhaps you were led astray by a solid distracter answer? Going back through your corrected test will give you a leg up on your next one by revealing your tendencies as to what you may be vulnerable with, in terms of multiple choice tests.

It may be a lot of extra work, but in the long run, going through your corrected multiple choice tests will work wonders for you in preparation for the real exam. See if you perhaps misread the question or even missed it because you were unprepared. Think of it like instant replays in professional sports. You are going back and looking at what you did on the big stage in the past so you can help fix and remedy any errors that could pose problems for you on the real exam.

CPSIA information can be obtained
at www.ICGtesting.com
Printed in the USA
LVHW102217170521
687714LV00026B/490